The Second Coming Of Christ
(Originally published in 1896)

By

Harriet Beecher Stowe
D. L. Moody
J. C. Ryle
George Muller
D. W. White
G. C. Needham
Charles H. Spurgeon
J. W.

****
AND
****

PLAN OF THE AGES: With Chart
(Originally published in 1893)

By

George C. Needham

Trumpet Press, Lawton, OK

Copyright © 2023 by Trumpet Press All rights reserved

No part of this book may be reproduced, stored in a retrieval system, or transmitted in any form or by any means, electronic, mechanical, recording or otherwise, without written permission by the copyright holder.

Library of Congress Catalog-in-Publication Data

Needham, Moody, Muller, Ryle, Spurgeon, Stowe, White
Title: The Second Coming Of Christ
1. Return of Christ 2. Rapture 3. Eschatology 4. Millennium

ISBN: 978-1-0882-0168-8

Trumpet Press is a member of the Christian Small Press Association.

If you see a mistake of any kind, such as a missing period or quotation mark, contact the publisher at trumpetpress77@gmail.com.

Book 1: *The Second Coming of Christ*
Table of Contents

Brief Preface 4

Chapter 1: He's Coming Tomorrow 5

Chapter 2: The Second Coming Of Christ 12

Chapter 3: Occupy Till I Come 23

Chapter 4: The Second Coming Of Christ 42

Chapter 5: The Second Coming Of Our Lord 53

Chapter 6: The Blessed Hope 66

Chapter 7: The Second Coming Of Christ 70

Chapter 8: The Missing Ones 85

Book 2: *Plan of The Ages; With Chart*
Table of Contents

Plan of The Ages 87

AGE FROM ADAM TO NOAH 95

AGE FROM NOAH TO ABRAHAM 96

AGE FROM ABRAHAM TO MOSES 97

AGE FROM MOSES TO NEBUCHADNEZZAR 98

NEBUCHADNEZZAR TO JESUS 99

AGE FROM CHRIST TO ANTICHRIST 101

AGE OF CHRIST'S MILLENNIAL KINGDOM 103

AGE OF THE PERFECT KINGDOM OF THE SON OF MAN ... 105

Publisher's Preface

I recently came across this book originally published in 1896. It has eight chapters, each one written by a well-known minister of the era, except the last chapter written by an unknown person with the initials J. W., who was likely well-known at the time.

Written for the layman, not the scholar, each chapter is in one way or another about the return of Christ. It is a very good book for anyone seeking to learn the basics of the second coming of Christ, called eschatology.

Even though I have written four books on Bible prophecy, I plan to read this book and add it to my library. (Michael D. Fortner, publisher)

> *This same Jesus which is taken up from you into heaven, shall so come in like manner as you have seen him go into heaven.* (Acts 1:11)

Originally published in 1896.

All content is the same as in the original, but the formatting has been updated for improved readability.

CHAPTER ONE

"HE'S COMING TOMORROW"

Mrs. Harriet Beecher Stowe

"The night is far spent; the day is at hand."

MY SOUL VIBRATED for a moment like a harp. Is it true? The night, the long night of the world's groping agony and blind desire, is it almost over? Is the day at hand?

"They shall see the Son of man coming in a cloud, with power and great glory. And when these things come to pass, look up and rejoice, for your redemption is nigh."

Coming!—The Son of man really coming into this world again with power and great glory?

Will this really ever happen? Will this solid, commonplace earth see it? Will these skies brighten and flash? and will upturned faces in this city be watching to see Him coming?

So our minister preached in a solemn sermon; and for moments, at times, I felt a thrill of reality in hearing. But, as the well-dressed crowd passed down the aisle, my neighbor Mr. Stockton whispered to me not to forget the meeting of the bank-directors on Monday evening. Mrs. Goldthwaite poured into my wife's ear a charge not to forget her party on Thursday; and my wife, as she came out, asked me if I had observed the extravagant outfit of Mrs. Rennyman.

"So absurd," she said, "when her income, I know, cannot be half what ours is! and I never think of sending to Paris for my things. I should look on it as morally wrong."

I spoke of the sermon.

"Yes," said my wife, "what a sermon!—so solemn. I wonder that all are not drawn to hear our rector. What could be more powerful than such discourses? My dear, by the way, don't forget to change Mary's opal ring for a diamond one. Dear me! the Christmas presents were all so on my mind, that I was thinking of them every now and then in church; and that was so wrong of me!"

"My dear," said I, "sometimes it seems to me as if all our life were unreal. We go to church, and the things that we hear are either true or false. If they are true, what things they are! For instance, these sermons. If we are looking for that coming, we ought to feel and live differently from what we do! Do we really believe what we hear in church? or is it a dream?"

"I do believe," said my wife earnestly — (she is a good woman, my wife) — "Yes, I do believe, but it is just as you say. Oh, dear! I feel as if I am very worldly—I have so many things to think of!" and she sighed.

So did I; for I knew that I, too, was very worldly. After a pause I said, "Suppose Christ should really come this Christmas and it should be authoritatively announced that He would be here tomorrow?"

"I think," said my wife, "there would be some embarrassment on the part of our great men, legislators, and chief councilors, in anticipation of a personal interview. Fancy a meeting of the city council to arrange a reception for the Lord Jesus Christ!"

"Perhaps," said I, "He would refuse all offers of the rich and great. Perhaps our fashionable churches would plead for His presence in vain. He would not be in palaces."

"Oh!" said my wife earnestly, "if I thought our money separates us from Him, I would give it all-- yes, all—might I only see Him."

She spoke from the bottom of her heart, and for a moment her face was glorified.

"You will see Him some day," said I, "and the money we are willing to give up at a word from Him will not keep Him from us."

That evening the thoughts of the waking hours mirrored themselves in a dream.

I seemed to be out walking in the streets, and to be conscious of a strange, vague sense of something just declared, of which all were speaking with a suppressed air of mysterious voices.

There was a whispering stillness around. Groups of men stood at the corners of the street, and discussed an impending something with suppressed voices.

I heard one say to another, "Really coming? What? Tomorrow?"

And the others said, "Yes, tomorrow. On Christmas Day He will be here."

It was night. The stars were glittering down with a keen and frosty light; the shops glistened in their Christmas array: but the same sense of hushed expectancy pervaded everything. There seemed to be nothing doing, and each person looked wistfully upon his neighbor, as if to say, "Have you heard?"

Suddenly, as I walked, an angel-form was with me, gliding softly by my side. The face was solemn, serene, and calm. Above the forehead was a pale, tremulous, phosphorous radiance of light, purer than any on earth—a light of quality so different from that of the street lamps that my celestial attendant seemed to move in a sphere alone.

Yet, though I felt awe, I felt a sort of confiding love as I said, "Tell me — is it really true? Is Christ coming?"

"He is," said the angel. "Tomorrow He will be here!"

"What joy!" I cried.

"Is it joy?" said the angel. "Alas, to many in this city it is only terror! Come with me."

In a moment I seemed to be standing with him in a parlor of one of the chief places of the city. A stout, florid, bald-headed man was seated at a table covered with papers, which he was sorting over with nervous anxiety, muttering to himself as he did so. On a sofa lay a sad-looking, delicate woman, her emaciated hands clasped over a little book. The room was, in all its appointments, a witness of boundless wealth. Gold and silver, and gems, and foreign furniture, and costly pictures, and articles of virtue — everything that money could buy, — were heaped together; and yet the man himself seemed to me to have been neither elevated nor refined by the confluence of all these treasures. He seemed nervous and uneasy. He wiped the sweat from his brow, and spoke, —

"I don't know, wife, how you feel; but I don't like this news. I don't understand it. It puts a stop to everything I know anything about."

"O John!" said the woman, turning toward him a face pale and fervent, and clasping her hands, "how can you say so?"

And, as she spoke, I could see breaking out above her head a tremulous light, like that above the brow of an angel.

"Well, Mary, it's the truth. I don't care if I say it. I don't want to meet—well, I wish He would put it off! What does He want of me? I'd be willing to make over—well, three millions to found a hospital, if He'd be satisfied and let me go on. Yes, I'd give three millions—to buy off from tomorrow."

"Is He not our best friend?"

"Best friend!" said the man, with a look half fright, half anger. "Mary, you don't know what you are talking about! You know I always hated those things. There's no use in it: I can't see into them. In fact, I hate them."

She cast on him a look full of pity. "Cannot I make you see?" she said.

"No, indeed, you can't. Why, look here," he added, pointing to the papers, "here is what stands for millions! Tonight it's mine; and tomorrow it will be all so much waste paper: and then what have I left? Do you think I can rejoice? I'd give half; I'd give — yes, the whole, not to have Him come these hundred years."

She stretched out her thin hand toward him; but he pushed it back.

"Do you see?" said the angel to me solemnly; "between him and her there is a 'great gulf fixed.' They have lived in one house with that gulf between them for years! She cannot go to him: he cannot come to her. Tomorrow she will rise to Christ as a dewdrop to the sun; and he will call to the mountains and rocks to fall on him, — not because Christ hates him, but because he hates Christ."

Again the scene was changed. We stood together in a little low attic, lighted by one small lamp, — how poor it was! — a broken chair, a rickety table, a bed in the corner where the little ones were cuddling close to one another for warmth. Poor things! the air was so frosty that their breath congealed upon the bedclothes, as they talked in soft, baby voices.

"When mother comes, she will bring us some supper," said they.

"But I'm so cold!" said the little outsider.

"Get in the middle, then," said the other two, "and we'll warm you. Mother promised she would make a fire when she came in, if that man would pay her."

"What a bad man he is!" said the oldest boy: "he never pays mother if he can help it."

Just then the door opened, and a pale, thin woman came in, laden with packages.

She laid all down, and came to her children's bed, clasping her hands in rapture.

"Joy! joy, children! Oh, joy, joy! Christ is coming! He will be here tomorrow."

Every little bird in the nest was up, and the little arms around the mother's neck: the children believed at once. They had heard of the good Jesus. He had been their mother's only Friend through, many a cold and hungry day, and they doubted not He was coming.

"O mother! will He take us? He will, won't He?"

"Yes, my little ones," she said softly, smiling to herself. "He shall gather the lambs with His arms, and carry them in His bosom."

Suddenly again, as if by the slide of a magic-lantern, another scene was present.

We stood in a lonely room, where a woman was sitting with her head bowed forward upon her hands. Alone, forsaken, slandered, she was in bitterness of spirit. Hard, cruel tongues had spoken her name with vile assertions, and a thoughtless world had believed. There had been a babble of accusations, a crowd to rejoice in iniquity, and few to pity. She thought herself alone, and she spoke: "Judge me, O Lord I for I have walked in my integrity. I am as a monster unto many; but Thou art my strong refuge."

In a moment the angel touched her. "My sister," he said, "be of good cheer. Christ will be here tomorrow."

She started up, with her hands clasped, her eyes bright, her whole form dilated, as she seemed to look into the heavens, and said with rapture,—

"Come, Lord, and judge me; for Thou knowest me altogether. Come, Son of man, in Thee have I trusted; let me never be confounded. Oh, for the judgment seat of Christ!"

Again I stood in a brilliant room, full of luxuries. Three or four fair women were standing pensively talking with each other. Their apartment was bestrewn with jewelry, laces, silks, velvets, and every fanciful elegance of fashion; but they looked troubled.

"This seems to me really awful," said one, with a suppressed sigh. "What troubles me is, I know so little about it."

"Yes," said another, "and it puts a stop to everything! Of what use will all these be tomorrow?"

There was a poor seamstress in the corner of the room, who now spoke.

"We shall be ever with the Lord," she said.

"I'm sure I don't know what that can mean," said the first speaker, with a kind of shudder; "it seems rather fearful."

"Well," said another, "it seems so sudden—when one never dreamed of any such thing—to change all at once from this to that other life."

"It is enough to *be with Him,*" said the poor woman. "Oh, I have so longed for it!"

"*The great gulf,*" again said the angel.

Then again we stood on the steps of a church. A band of clergymen were together. Episcopalian, Methodist, Congregationalist, Baptist, Presbyterian, Old School and New School, all stood hand in hand.

"It's no matter now about these old issues," they said. "*He* is coming: He will settle all. Ordinations and ordinances, sacraments and creeds, are but the scaffolding of the edifice. They are the shadow: the substance is CHRIST!" And hand in hand they turned their faces when the Christmas morning light began faintly glowing; and I heard them saying together, with one heart and voice,—

"Come, LORD JESUS! come quickly!"

CHAPTER TWO

THE SECOND COMING OF CHRIST

D. L. Moody

Study of Prophecy—Three Great Comings—The Stone Cut out of the Mountain—How will He Come?—When?—Watch!—Not at Death —The Order of Events—For Young Converts—At the Communion Table—The Millennium—No Universal Conversion — Reunion with Friends—The Oft-repeated Promise and Prayer

IN SECOND TIMOTHY, third chapter, verse sixteen, Paul declares: "All Scripture is given by inspiration of God, and is profitable for doctrine, for reproof, for correction, for instruction in righteousness."

But there are some people who tell us, when we take up prophecy, that it is all very well to be believed, but that there is no use in one trying to understand it; that future events are things that the Church does not agree about, and it is better to let them alone, and deal only with those prophecies which have already been fulfilled.

But Paul doesn't talk that way; he says: "ALL Scripture is . . . profitable for doctrine." If these people are right, he ought to have said: "Some Scripture is profitable; but you can't understand the prophecies, so you had better let them alone." If God did not mean to have us study the prophecies, He would not have put them into the Bible. Some of them are fulfilled, and He is fulfilling the rest, so that if we do not see them all completed in this life, we shall in the world to come. Prophecy, as has been said, is the mold in which history is cast. About one-third of the Bible is prophetical, and a large portion of the remainder is typical of things that were to come.

Three great comings are foretold in the Word of God.

* First, that Christ should come; that has been fulfilled.

* Secondly, that the Holy Ghost should come; that was fulfilled at Pentecost, and the Church is able to testify to it by its experience of His saving grace.

* Third, the return of our Lord from Heaven —for this we are told to watch and wait "till He come."

I do not want to teach anything dogmatically, on my own authority; but to my mind this precious doctrine—for such I must call it—of the return of the Lord to this earth is taught in the New Testament as clearly as any other doctrine in it. If you read the twenty-sixth chapter of Matthew, the sixty-fourth verse, you will find that it was just this very thing that caused His death. When the high priests asked Him who He was, and if He was the true Messiah, what does He reply:

"I say unto you, Hereafter shall ye see the Son of man sitting on the right hand of power, and coming in the clouds of heaven."

That was enough. The moment they heard that, they accused Him of blasphemy, and condemned Him to death, just because He said He was coming again.

Whoever neglects this has only a mutilated Gospel, for the Bible teaches us not only of the death and sufferings of Christ, but also of His return to reign in honor and glory. His second coming is mentioned and referred to over three hundred times, yet I was in the Church fifteen or sixteen years before I ever heard a sermon on it. There is hardly any church that does not make a great deal of baptism, but in all of Paul's epistles I believe baptism is spoken of only thirteen times, while he speaks about the return of our Lord fifty times; and yet the Church has had very little to say about it. Now, I can see a reason for this;

THE DEVIL DOES NOT WANT US TO SEE THIS TRUTH

for nothing would wake up the Church so much. The moment a man realizes that Jesus Christ is coming back again to receive His followers to Himself, this world loses its hold upon him. Gas stocks and water stocks and stocks in banks and railroads are of very much less consequence to him then. His heart is free, and he looks for the blessed appearing of His Lord, who, at His coming, will take him into His blessed Kingdom.

Some people say, "The prophecies are all well enough for the priests and clergy, but not for the rank and file of the Church."

But Peter says, "The prophecy came not by the will of man, but holy men of God spake as they were moved by the Holy Ghost," and those men are the very ones who tell us of the return of our Lord.

Look at Daniel, where he tells the meaning of that stone which King Nebuchadnezzar saw in his dream, that was cut out of the mountain without hands, and that broke in pieces the iron, the brass, the clay, the silver, and the gold.

"The dream is certain, and the interpretation thereof sure," says Daniel. Now, we have seen the fulfillment of that prophecy, all but the closing part of it. The kingdoms of Babylon and Medo-Persia and Greece and Rome have all been broken in pieces, and now it only remains for this stone, cut out of the mountain without hands, to smite the image and break it in pieces till it becomes like the dust of the summer threshing floor, and for this stone to become a great mountain and fill the whole earth.

BUT HOW WILL HE COME?

We are told how He is going to come. When the disciples stood looking up into heaven at the time of His ascension, there appeared two angels, who said unto them (Acts first chapter, verse eleven): "Ye men of Galilee, why stand ye gazing up into heaven? This same Jesus which is taken up from you into heaven shall so come in like manner as ye have seen Him go into heaven."

How did He go up? He took His flesh and bones up with Him. *"Look at me; handle me; a spirit has not flesh and bones as ye see me have. I am the identical one whom they crucified and laid in the grave. Now I am risen from the dead and am going up to heaven."*

"He is gone," say the angels, "but He will come again just as He went."

An angel was sent to announce His birth to the Virgin. Angels sang of His advent in Bethlehem. An angel told the women of His resurrection. Two angels told the disciples of His coming again. It is the same testimony in all these cases.

I do not know why people should not like to study the Bible, and find out all about this precious doctrine of our Lord's return. Some have gone beyond prophecy, and tried to tell the very day He would come. Perhaps that is one reason why people don't believe this doctrine. He is coming— we know that; but just when He is coming we don't know. Matthew settles that: "But of that day and hour knoweth no man, no, not the angels of heaven, but my Father only." The angels don't know. It is something the Father keeps to Himself.

In Luke we read: "The Son of man cometh at an hour when ye think not."

McCheyne, the Scottish preacher, once said to some friends, "Do you think Christ will come tonight?"

One after another they said, "I think not."

When all had given this answer, he solemnly repeated this text: "The Son of man cometh at an hour *when ye think not*."

Commenting on the text: "It is not for you to know the times or the seasons, which the Father hath put in His own power," Spurgeon said: "If I were introduced into a room where a large number of parcels were stored up, and I was told that there was something good for me, I should begin to look for that which had my name upon it, and when I came upon a parcel and I saw in pretty big letters, '*It is not for you*,' I should leave it alone. Here, then, is a casket of knowledge marked, '*It is not for you* to know the times or the seasons, which the Father hath put in His own power.'

"Cease to meddle with matters which are concealed, and be satisfied to know the things which are clearly revealed."

If Christ had said, "I will not come back for 2,000 years," none of His disciples would have begun to watch for Him until the time was near, but it is THE PROPER ATTITUDE OF A CHRISTIAN to be always looking for his Lord's return. So God does not tell us when Christ is to come, but He tells us to watch. Just as Simeon and Anna watched and waited for His first coming, so should true believers watch and wait for His return. It is not enough to say you are a Christian, and that you are all right. You are not all right unless you obey the command to watch.

We find also that He is to come unexpectedly and suddenly. "For as the lightning cometh out of the east and shineth unto the west, even so shall also the coming of the Son of man be." And again, "Therefore be ye also ready, for in such an hour as ye think not the Son of man cometh."

Some people say that means death; but the Word of God does not say it means death. Death is our enemy, but our Lord has the keys of Death. He has conquered death, Hell and the grave, and at any moment He may come to set us free from death, and destroy our last enemy for us.

In the last chapter of John there is a text that seems to settle this matter. Peter asks the question about John, "Lord, what shall this man do? Jesus said unto him, If I will that he tarry *till I come*, what is that to thee? Follow thou me. Then went this saying abroad among the brethren that that disciple *should not die*."

They did not think that the coming of the Lord meant death; there was a great difference between these two things in their minds. Christ is the Prince of Life. There is no death where He is. Death flees at His coming. Dead bodies sprang to life when He touched them or spoke to them. His coming is not death, He is the resurrection and the life. When He sets up His kingdom, there is to be no death, but life forevermore.

Look at that account of the last hours of Christ with His disciples. What does He say to them? "If I go away I will send death after you to bring you to Me" or "I will send an angel after you?" Not at all. He says: "I will come again and receive you unto Myself."

It is this that makes the fourteenth chapter of John so sweet.

There is another mistake, as you will find if you read your Bibles carefully. Some think that at the second coming of Christ everything is to be brought about in a few minutes, but I do not so understand it. THE FIRST THING HE IS TO DO is to take His Church out of the world. He calls the Church His bride, and He says He is going to prepare a place for her.

We may judge, says one, what a glorious place it will be from the length of time He is in preparing it, and when the place is ready He will come and take the Church to Himself. In the closing verses of the fourth chapter of I Thessalonians, Paul says:

"If we believe that Jesus died and rose again, even so them also which sleep in Jesus will God bring with Him . . . We which are alive and remain unto the coming of the Lord shall not prevent them which are asleep. For the Lord Himself shall descend from heaven with a shout, with the voice of the archangel, and with the trump of God, and the dead in Christ shall rise first. Then we which are alive and remain shall be caught up together with them in the clouds to meet the Lord in the air, and so shall we ever be with the Lord. Wherefore, comfort one another with these words." That is the comfort of the Church.

If my wife were in a foreign country, and I had a beautiful mansion all ready for her, she would a good deal rather I should come and bring her to it than to have me send someone else to bring her. He has prepared a mansion for His bride, the Church, and He promises for our joy and comfort that HE WILL COME HIMSELF and bring us to the place He has been all this while preparing.

There was a time when I used to mourn that I should not be alive in the millennium; but now I EXPECT TO BE IN THE MILLENNIUM.

Dean Alford says —and almost everybody bows to him in the matter of interpretation— that he must insist that this coming of Christ to take His Church to Himself in the clouds, is not the same event as His coming to judge the world at the last day. The deliverance of the Church is one thing, judgment is another. Christ will save His Church, but He will save them finally by taking them out of the world.

Some may shake your heads and say: "Oh, well, that is too deep for the most of us. Such things ought not to be said before young converts. Only the very wisest characters, such as the ministers and the professors in the theological seminaries, can understand them."

But, my friends, Paul wrote about these things to the young converts among the Thessalonians, and he told them to comfort one another with these words. Here in the first chapter of I Thessalonians Paul says: "Ye turned to God from idols to serve the living and true God, and to wait for His Son from heaven, whom He raised from the dead, even Jesus, which delivered us from the wrath to come."

To wait for His Son—that is the true attitude of every child of God. If he is doing that, he is ready for the duties of life, ready for God's work; yes, that makes him feel that he is just ready to begin to work for God.

Then over in the next chapter he says: "For what is our hope, or joy, or crown of rejoicing? Are not even ye, in the presence of our Lord Jesus Christy at His coming?" And again, in the third chapter, thirteenth verse: "To the end that He may establish your hearts unblameable in holiness before God, even our Father, at the coming of our Lord Jesus Christ with all His saints." Still again, in the fifth chapter and twenty-third verse: "I pray God your whole spirit and soul and body be preserved blameless unto the coming of our Lord Jesus Christ."

He has something to say about this same thing in every chapter; indeed, I have thought this Epistle to the Thessalonians might be called the Gospel of Christ's Coming Again.

Take the account of the words of Christ at the communion table. It seems to me the devil has covered up the most precious thing about it. "For as often as ye eat this bread and drink this cup, ye do show forth the Lord's death *till He come*." But most people seem to think that the Lord's table is the place for self-examination, and repentance, and making good resolutions. Not at all; they spoil it that way. It is to show forth the Lord's death, and we are to observe it till He comes.

Some people say, "I believe Christ will come on the other side of the millennium."

Where do they get it? I can't find it. The Word of God nowhere tells me to watch and wait for signs of the coming of the millennium, (such as the return of the Jews,) but for the coming of the Lord; to be ready at midnight to meet Him, like those five wise virgins.

At one time I thought the world would grow better and better until Christ could stay away no longer; but in studying the Bible I don't find any place where God says so, or that Christ is to have a spiritual reign on earth of a thousand years. I find that

THE WORLD IS TO GROW WORSE AND WORSE, and that at length there is going to be a separation. The Church is to be translated out of the world, and of this we have two examples already, two representatives (as we might say) in Christ's Kingdom, of what is to be done for all His true believers. Enoch is the representative of the first dispensation, Elijah of the second, and, as a representative of the third dispensation, we have the Savior Himself, who entered into the heavens for us, and became the first-fruits of them that slept. We are not to wait for the great white throne judgment, but the glorified Church is set on the throne with Christ, and to help to judge the world.

Now, some think this is a new and strange doctrine, and that they who preach it are speckled birds. But let me say that many spiritual men in the pulpits of Great Britain, as well as in this country, are firm in this faith. Spurgeon preached it. I have heard Newman Hall say that he knew no reason why Christ might not come before he got through with his sermon. But in certain churches, where they have the form of godliness, but deny the power thereof—just the state of things which Paul declares shall be in the last days—this doctrine is not preached or believed.

They do not want sinners to cry out in their meetings, "What must I do to be saved?"

They want intellectual preachers who will cultivate their taste, brilliant preachers who will rouse their imagination, but they don't want the preaching that has in it the power of the Holy Ghost. We live in the day of SHAMS IN RELIGION.

The Church is cold and formal; may God wake us up! And I know of no better way to do it than to get the Church to look for the return of our Lord.

Some people say, "Oh, you will discourage the young converts if you preach that doctrine."

Well, my friends, that hasn't been my experience. I have felt like working three times as hard ever since I came to understand that my Lord was coming back again.

The Second Coming Of Christ

I look on this world as a wrecked vessel. God has given me a lifeboat, and said to me, "Moody, save all you can." God will come in judgment to this world, but the children of God don't belong to this world; they are in it, but not of it, like a ship in the water; and their greatest danger is not the opposition of the world, but their own conformity to the world. This world is getting darker and darker; its ruin is coming nearer and nearer; if you have any friends on this wreck unsaved, you had better lose no time in getting them off.

But someone will say, "Do you then make the grace of God a failure?"

No; grace is not a failure, but man is. The antediluvian world was a failure. The Jewish world was a failure. Man has been a failure everywhere when he has had his own way and been left to himself. When the Son of God left Heaven, and came to this sin-cursed earth to open up a new and living way whereby we might return to God, the earth would give Him no better quarters than a manger for His birthplace, no place to lay His head during the years of His ministry, and only the cruel cross in His death.

Nowhere in the Scriptures is it claimed that the whole world shall be brought to the feet of Christ in this dispensation. In the fifteenth chapter of Acts, James says: "Simeon hath declared how God at the first did visit the Gentiles, to take out of them a people for His name." That is one reason for our Lord's delay. He is waiting until the elect are all gathered out, until His Gentile bride is complete.

Now, don't take my word for it. Look this doctrine up in your Bibles, and, if you find it there, bow down to it, and receive it as the Word of God. Take Matthew, twenty-fourth chapter, verse fifty: "The Lord of that servant shall come in a day when he looketh not for him, and in a hour that he is not aware of, and shall cut him asunder, and appoint him his portion with the hypocrites; there shall be weeping and gnashing of teeth."

Take II Peter, third chapter, fourth and fifth verses: "There shall come in the last days scoffers, walking after their own lusts, and saying, Where is the promise of His coming? for since the fathers fell asleep, all things continue as they were from the beginning of the creation." Go out on the streets, and ask men about the return of our Lord, and that is just what they would say:

"Ah, yes; the Lord delayeth His coming! I don't propose to trouble myself about it. It will not be in my day."

But Peter goes on to say, verse ten: "But the day of the Lord will come as a thief in the night; in the which the heavens shall pass away with a great noise, and the elements shall melt with fervent heat; the earth also and the works that are therein shall be burned up." We have no right then to say when it will not come, any more than we have to say when it will come. As someone has said, Christ's second coming does not occur so quickly as impatience, nor yet so late as carelessness, supposes.

There is another thought I want to bring to your attention, and that is: Christ will bring our friends with Him when He comes. All who have died in the Lord are to be with Him when He descends from His Father's throne into the air.

An interval of time ensues between this meeting of all His saints in the air and His coming with all His saints to execute judgment upon the ungodly, to chain Satan in the bottomless pit for the thousand years, and to establish the millennial reign in great power and glory.

"Blessed and holy is he that hath part in the first resurrection; on such the second death has no power, but they shall be priests of God and of Christ, and shall reign with Him a thousand years." "But the rest of the dead lived not again until the thousand years were past; this is the first resurrection."

That looks as if the Church was to reign a thousand years with Christ before the final judgment of the great White Throne, when Satan shall be cast into the Lake of Fire, and there shall be new heavens and a new earth.

When Christ returns, He will not be treated as He was before. There will be room for Him at Bethlehem. He will be welcome in Jerusalem. He will reveal Himself as Joseph revealed himself to his brethren. He will say to the Jews, "I am Jesus," and they will reply: "Blessed is He that cometh in the name of the Lord." And the Jews will then be that nation that shall be born in a day.

"Behold, I come quickly," said Christ to John. Three times it is repeated in the last chapter of the Bible. And almost the closing words of the Bible are the prayer: "Even so, come, Lord Jesus."

Were the early Christians disappointed, then? No; no man is disappointed who obeys the voice of God. The world waited for the first coming of the Lord, waited for 4,000 years, and then He came. He was here only thirty-three years, and then He went away. But He left us a promise that He would come again; and, as the world watched and waited for His first coming and did not watch in vain, so now, to them who wait for His appearing, shall He appear a second time unto salvation.

Now, let the question go round, "Am I ready to meet the Lord if He comes tonight?"

"Be ye also ready, for in such an hour as ye think not the Son of Man cometh."

CHAPTER THREE

"OCCUPY TILL I COME"

J C. Ryle

The Parable of the Pounds—The Mistake of the Disciples Our Parallel Mistake—The Fulfillment of Prophecy —The Present Position of our Lord—What He will Do on His return—The Present Dispensation—The Present Duty of Christians—Warning—Question—Invitation—Exhortation

> And as they heard these things, He added and spake a parable, because He was nigh to Jerusalem, and because they thought that the kingdom of God should immediately appear.
>
> He said therefore, A certain nobleman went into a far country to receive for himself a kingdom, and to return.
>
> And he called his ten servants, and delivered them ten pounds, and said unto them, *Occupy till I come*. (Luke 19:11-13)

READER, the words before your eyes form an introduction to the parable, which is commonly called the "Parable of the Pounds." They contain matter which deserves the prayerful consideration of every true Christian.

There are some parables of which Matthew Henry says, with equal quaintness and truth, "The key hangs beside the door." The Holy Ghost Himself interprets them. There is no room left for doubt as to the purpose for which they were spoken. Of such parables the parable of the Pounds is an example.

Luke tells us that our Lord Jesus Christ "*added and spake a parable, because He was nigh to Jerusalem, and because they thought that the kingdom of God should immediately appear.*"

These words reveal to us the secret thoughts of our Lord's disciples at this period of His ministry. They were drawing nigh to Jerusalem. They gathered from many of their Master's sayings that something remarkable was about to happen. They had a strong impression that one great end of His coming into the world was about to be accomplished. So far they were quite right. As to the precise nature of the event about to happen they were quite wrong.

Reader, there are three subjects opened up in this passage of Scripture which appear to me to be of the deepest importance. Upon each of these I wish to offer a few thoughts for your private meditation. I purposely abstain from touching any part of the parable except the beginning. I want to direct your attention to the three following points:

I. I will speak of the mistake of the disciples, referred to in the verses before us.

II. I will speak of the present position of the Lord Jesus Christ.

III. I will speak of the present duty of all who profess to be Jesus Christ's disciples.

May God bless the reading to everyone into whose hands this may fall. May every reader be taught to pray that the Spirit will guide him into all truth.

I. THE MISTAKE INTO WHICH THE DISCIPLES HAD FALLEN

What was this mistake? Let us try to understand this point clearly.

Our Lord's disciples seem to have thought that the Old Testament promises of Messiah's visible kingdom and glory were about to be immediately fulfilled. They believed rightly that He was indeed the Messiah, the Christ of God; but they blindly supposed that He was going at once to take to Himself His great power, and to reign gloriously over the earth. This was the sum and substance of their error.

They appear to have concluded that now was the day and now the hour-- when the Redeemer would build up Zion, and appear in

His glory, when He would smite the earth with the rod of His mouth, and with the breath of His lips slay the wicked, when He would assemble the outcasts of Israel, and gather the dispersed of Judah, when He would take the heathen for His inheritance, and the uttermost parts of the earth for His possession, break His enemies with a rod of iron, and dash them in pieces like a potter's vessel, when He would reign in Mount Zion and in Jerusalem, and before His ancients gloriously, when the kingdom and dominion and the greatness of the kingdom under the whole heaven would be given to the saints of the Most High.

Such appears to have been the mistake, into which our Lord's disciples had fallen at the time when He spoke the parable of the Pounds.

It was a *great mistake* unquestionably. They did not realize that before all these prophecies could be fulfilled, "it behooved Christ to suffer." Their sanguine expectations overleaped the crucifixion and the long parenthesis of time to follow, and bounded onward to the final glory.

They did not see that there was to be a first advent of Messiah "to be cut off," before the second advent of Messiah to reign. They did not perceive that the sacrifices and ceremonies of the law of Moses were first to receive their fulfillment in a better sacrifice and a better High Priest, and a shedding of blood more precious than that of bulls and goats.

They did not comprehend that before the glory Christ must be crucified, and an elect people gathered out from among the Gentiles by the preaching of the Gospel. All these were dark things to them. They grasped part of the prophetical word, but not all.

They saw that Christ was to have a kingdom, but they did not see that He was to be wounded and bruised, and be an offering for sin. They understood the dispensation of the crown and the glory, but not the dispensation of the cross and the shame. Such was their mistake.

I believe we have fallen into an error parallel with that of our Jewish brethren,—an error less fatal in its consequences than theirs, but an error far more inexcusable because we have had more light.

If the Jew thought too exclusively of Christ reigning, has not the Gentile thought too exclusively of Christ suffering?

If the Jew could see nothing in Old Testament prophecy but Christ's exaltation and final power, has not the Gentile often seen nothing but Christ's humiliation and the preaching of the Gospel? If the Jew dwelt too much on Christ's second advent, has not the Gentile dwelt too exclusively on the first? If the Jew ignored the cross, has not the Gentile ignored the crown?

I believe there can be but one answer to these questions. I believe that we Gentiles have been very guilty concerning a large portion of God's truth. I believe that we have cherished an arbitrary, reckless habit of interpreting first advent texts literally, and second advent texts spiritually. I believe we have not rightly understood "all that the Prophets have spoken" about the second personal advent of Christ, any more than the Jews did about the first.

Reader, I earnestly invite your special attention to the point on which I am now dwelling. I know not what your opinions may be about the fulfillment of the prophetical parts of Scripture, but I ask you in all affection to examine your views. I entreat you to consider calmly whether your opinions about Christ's second advent and kingdom are as sound and scriptural as those of His first disciples. I entreat you to take heed, lest insensibly you commit as great error about Christ's second coming and glory, as they did about Christ's first coming and cross.

Throw aside all prejudice, and view the subject with calm and dispassionate thought. Take up anew the prophetical Scriptures, and pray that you may not err in interpreting their meaning. Read them in the light of those two great polestars, the first and second advents of Jesus Christ. Bind up with the first advent the rejection of the Jews, the calling of the Gentiles, the preaching of the Gospel as a witness to the world, and the gathering out of the election of grace. Bind up with the Second Advent the restoration of the Jews, the pouring out of judgments on unbelieving Gentiles, the conversion of the world, and the establishment of Christ's kingdom upon earth. Do this, and you will see a meaning and fullness in prophecy which perhaps you have never discovered.

It is time for Christians to *interpret unfulfilled prophecy by the light of prophecies already fulfilled*. The curses on the Jews were brought to pass literally:—so also will be the blessings. The scattering was literal: so also will be the gathering.

The pulling down of Zion was literal:—so also will be the building up. The rejection of Israel was literal:—so also will be the restoration.

It is high time to *interpret the events that shall accompany Christ's Second Advent by the light of those accompanying His first advent*. The first advent was literal, visible, personal:—so also will be His second. His first advent was with a literal body:—so also will be His second. At His first advent the least predictions were fulfilled to the very letter:—so also will they be at His second. The shame was literal and visible:—so also will be the glory.

It is high time to *cease from explaining Old Testament prophecies in a way not warranted by the New Testament*. What right have we to say that the words Judah, Zion, Israel, and Jerusalem, ever mean anything but literal Judah, literal Zion, literal Israel and literal Jerusalem? What precedent shall we find in the New Testament? Hardly any, if indeed any at all. Well says an admirable writer on this subject:—

> "There are really only two or three places in the whole New Testament—Gospels, Epistles, and Revelation—where such names are used decidedly in what may be called a spiritual or figurative state. The word 'Jerusalem' occurs eighty times, and all of them unquestionably literal, save when the opposite is expressly pointed out by the epithets 'heavenly,' or 'new,' or 'holy.' 'Jew' occurs an hundred times, and only four are even ambiguous. 'Israel' and 'Israelite' occur forty times, and all literal. 'Judah' and 'Judea' above twenty times, and all literal."

II. WHAT IS THE PRESENT POSITION OF OUR LORD JESUS CHRIST?

The parable appears to me to answer that question distinctly in the twelfth verse. "A certain nobleman went into a far country to receive for himself a kingdom, and to return." This nobleman represents the Lord Jesus Christ, and that in two respects.

Like the nobleman, the Lord Jesus is gone into a far country to receive for Himself a kingdom. He has not received it yet in possession, though He has it in promise. He has a spiritual kingdom unquestionably. He is king over the hearts of His believing people, and they are all His faithful subjects. He has a controlling power over the world. He is King of kings and Lord of lords. "By Him all things consist," and nothing can happen without His permission. But His real, literal, visible, complete kingdom the Lord Jesus has not yet received.

"We see not yet all things put under Him." "He sits on the right hand of the Father till His enemies are made His footstool."

The devil is the prince of this world during the present dispensation. The vast majority of the inhabitants of the earth choose the things that please the devil far more than the things that please God. Little as they may think it, they are doing the devil's will, behaving as the devil's subjects, and serving the devil far more than Christ. This is the actual condition of Christendom as well as of heathen countries. After 1900 years of Bibles and Gospel preaching, there is not a nation, or a country, or a parish, or a long-established congregation, where the devil has not more subjects than Christ. So fearfully true is it that the world is not yet the kingdom of Christ.

The Lord Jesus during the present dispensation is like David between the time of his anointing and Saul's death. He has the promise of the kingdom, but He has not yet received the crown and throne. He is followed by a few, and those often neither great nor wise; but they are a faithful people. He is persecuted by His enemies, and ofttimes driven into the wilderness; and yet His party is never quite destroyed.

But He has none of the visible signs of the kingdom at present, —no earthly glory, majesty, greatness, obedience. The vast majority of mankind see no beauty in Him. They will not have this Man to reign over them. His people are not honored for their Master's sake. They walk the earth like princes in disguise. His kingdom is not yet come. His will is not yet done on earth excepting by a little flock. It is not the day of "His power." The Lord Jesus is biding His time.

But just as the Lord Jesus, like the nobleman, "went to receive a kingdom"; so, like the nobleman, the Lord Jesus intends one day "to return."

The words of the angels shall have a complete fulfillment: "This same Jesus which was taken up from you into heaven, shall so come in like manner as ye have seen Him go into heaven." As His going away was a real literal going away, so His return shall be a real literal return. As He came personally the first time with a body, so He shall come personally the second time with a body. As He came visibly to this earth and visibly went away, so when He comes the second time He shall visibly return. And then, and not till then, the complete kingdom of Christ shall begin. He left His servants as "a nobleman"; He returns to His servants as "a king."

Then He intends to cast out that old usurper the devil, to bind him for a thousand years, and to strip him of his power.

Then He intends to make a restitution of the face of creation. It shall be the world's jubilee day. Our earth shall at last bring forth her increase. The King shall at length have His own again. At last the ninety-seventh Psalm shall be fulfilled, and men shall say, "The Lord reigneth: let the earth rejoice!"

Then He intends to fulfill the prophecies of Enoch, John the Baptist, and Paul, "To execute judgment upon all the ungodly" inhabitants of Christendom—"to burn up the chaff with unquenchable fire" — and "in flaming fire to take vengeance on them that know not God, and obey not the Gospel."

Then He intends to raise His dead saints and gather His living ones, to gather together the scattered tribes of Israel, and to set up an empire on earth in which every knee shall bow to Him, and "every tongue confess that Christ is Lord."

When, how, where, in what manner, all these things shall be, we cannot say particularly. It is enough for us to know that they shall be. The Lord Jesus has undertaken to do them, and they shall be performed. The Lord Jesus waits for the time appointed by the Father, and then shall they all come to pass. As surely as He was born of a pure virgin, and lived on earth thirty-three years as a servant, so surely He shall come with clouds in glory, and reign on the earth as a King.

Reader, I charge you to establish in your mind, among the great verities of your religion, that Christ is one day to have a complete kingdom in this world, —that His kingdom is not yet set up,—but that it will be set up in the day of His return.

> Know clearly whose kingdom it is now: not Christ's, but the usurper Satan's.
> Know clearly whose kingdom it is to be one day: not Satan the usurper's, but Jesus Christ's.
> Know clearly when the kingdom is to change hands, and the usurper to be cast out: when the Lord Jesus returns in person, and not before.
> Know clearly what the Lord Jesus is doing now: He is sitting at the right hand of the Father.

He is interceding, as a High Priest in the holy of holies for His people,—adding to their number such as shall be saved by the preaching of the Gospel,—and waiting till the appointed "day of His power," when He shall come forth to bless His people, and sit as "a priest upon His throne." Know these things clearly, and you will do well.

Know these things clearly, and then *you will not cherish extravagant expectations* from any church, minister, or religious machinery in this present dispensation.

> You will not marvel to see ministers and missionaries not converting all to whom they preach.
> You will not wonder to find that while some believe the Gospel, many believe not.
> You will not be depressed and cast down when you see the children of the world in every place many, and the children of God few.

You will remember that "the days are evil," and that the time of general conversion has not yet arrived. You will thank God that any are converted at all, and that while the gospel is hid from the wise and prudent, it is yet revealed to babes. Alas for the man who expects a millennium before the Lord Jesus returns! How can this possibly be, if the world in the day of His coming is to be found as it was in the day of Noah and Lot?

Know these things clearly, and then *you will not be confounded and surprised by the continuance of immense evils in the world.* Wars, and tumults, and oppression, and dishonesty, and selfishness, and covetousness, and superstition, and bad government, and abounding heresies, will not appear to you unaccountable.

> You will not sink down into a morbid, misanthropic condition of mind when you see laws and reforms and education not making mankind perfect.

> You will not relapse into a state of apathy and disgust when you see churches full of imperfections, and theologians making mistakes.

> You will say to yourself, "The time of Christ's power has not yet arrived—the devil is still working among his children, and sowing darkness and division broadcast among the saints—the true King is yet to come."

Know these things clearly, and then *you will see why God delays the final glory,* and allows things to go on as they do in this world. It is not that He is not able to prevent evil, it is not that He is slack in the fulfilling of His promises, — but the Lord is taking out for Himself a people by the preaching of the Gospel. He is long-suffering to the unconverted.

> *"The Lord is not willing that any should perish, but that all should come to repentance."*

Once let the number of the elect be gathered out of the world,—once let the last elect sinner be brought to repentance,—and then the kingdom of Christ shall be set up, and the throne of grace shall be exchanged for the throne of glory.

Know these things clearly, and then you will *work diligently to do good to souls.* The time is short. "The night is far spent. The day is at hand." The signs of the times call loudly for watchfulness, and speak with no uncertain voice. The Turkish empire is drying up. The Jews are cared for as they never have been for hundreds of years. The Gospel is being preached as a witness in almost every corner of the world. Surely if we would pluck a few more brands from the burning before it is too late, we must work hard and lose no time. We must preach—we must warn—we must exhort—we must give money to religious societies—we must spend and be spent far more than we have ever done yet.

Know these things clearly, and then *you will be often looking for the coming of the day of God*. You will regard the Second Advent as a glorious and comfortable truth, around which your best hopes will all be clustered.

> You will not merely think of Christ crucified, but will think also of Christ's coming again.
>
> You will long for the days of refreshing and the manifestation of the sons of God.
>
> You will find peace in looking back to the cross, and you will find joyful hope in looking forward to the kingdom.

Once more, I repeat, know clearly Christ's present position. He is like one who is "gone into a far country to receive a kingdom, and then to return."

III. WHAT IS THE PRESENT DUTY OF ALL CHRIST'S PROFESSING DISCIPLES?

When I speak of present duty, I mean of course their duty between the period of Christ's first and second advents. And I find an answer in the words of the nobleman, in the parable, to his servants: "He delivered them ten pounds, and said unto them, Occupy till I come."

Reader, I know few words more searching and impressive than these four, "Occupy till I come."

> They are spoken to all who profess and call themselves Christians.
>
> They address the conscience of everyone who has not formally turned his back on Christianity.
>
> They ought to stir up all hearers of the Gospel to examine themselves whether they are in the faith, and to prove themselves.

For your sake, remember, these words were written: "Occupy till I come."

The Lord Jesus bids you "occupy." By that He means that you are to be "a doer" in your Christianity, and not merely a hearer and professor. He wants His servants not only to receive His wages, and eat His bread, and dwell in His house, and belong to His family,—but also to do His work. You are to "let your light so shine before men that they may see your good works."

Have you faith? It must not be a dead faith; it must "work by love."

Are you elect? You are elect unto "obedience."

Are you redeemed? You are redeemed that you may be "a peculiar people, zealous of good works."

Do you love Christ? Prove the reality of your love by keeping Christ's commandments.

Oh! Reader, do not forget this charge to "occupy." Beware of an idle, talking, gossiping, sentimental, do-nothing religion. Think not because your doings cannot justify you, or put away one single sin, that therefore it matters not whether you do anything at all. Away with such a delusion! Cast it behind you as an invention of the devil. Think of the house built upon the sand, and its miserable end. As ever you would "make your calling and election sure," be a doing Christian.

But the Lord Jesus also bids you *"occupy your pound."* By this He means that He has given each one of His people some opportunity of glorifying Him. He would have you understand that everyone has got his own sphere,—the poorest as well as the richest,—that everyone has an open door before him, and may, if he will, show forth his Master's praise.

Your bodily health and strength,

Your mental gifts and capacities,

Your money and your earthly possessions,

Your rank and position in life,

Your example and influence with others

Your liberty to read the Bible, and hear the Gospel,

Your plentiful supply of means of grace.

All these are your "pounds." All these are to be used and employed with a continual reference to the glory of Christ. All these are His gifts.

But the Lord Jesus bids you also to occupy till He comes. By that He means that you are to do His work on earth like one who continually looks for His return. You are to be like the faithful servant, who knows not what hour his master may come home, but keeps all things in readiness, and is always prepared. You are to be like one who knows that Christ's coming is the great reckoning day, and to be ready to render up your account at any moment. You are not to suppose that you have any freehold in this world, not even a lease.

The greatest and the richest of mankind is only God's tenant-at-will.

> You are not to neglect any social duty or relation of life because of the uncertainty of the Lord's return.
>
> You are to fill the station to which God has called you in a godly and Christian way;
>
> You are to be ready to go from the place of business to meet Christ in the air, if the Lord shall think fit.
>
> You are to be like a man who never knows what a day might bring forth, and, therefore, you are to put off nothing till a *"convenient season."*
>
> You are to rise and go forth in the morning ready, if need be, to meet Christ at noon.
>
> You are to lie down in bed at night ready, if need be, to be awakened by the midnight cry, "Behold the Bridegroom cometh."
>
> You are to keep your spiritual accounts in a state of constant preparation, like one who never knows how soon they may be called for.
>
> You are to measure all your ways by the measure of Christ's appearing, and to do nothing in which you would not like Jesus to find you engaged. This is to "occupy" till Jesus comes.

Think, reader, how *condemning* are these words to thousands of professing Christians! What an utter absence of preparation appears in their daily walk and conversation! How thoroughly unfit they are to meet Christ!

> They know nothing of occupying the gifts of God as loans for which they must give account.
>
> They show not the slightest desire to glorify Him with "body and spirit, which are His."
>
> They give no sign of readiness for the second advent.

Well says old Gurnall, "It may be written on the grave of every unconverted man. Here lies one who never did for God an hour's work."

Think again how *arousing* these words ought to be to all who are rich in this world, but do not know how to spend their money rightly. Alas! There are many who live on as if Christ had never said anything about the difficulty of rich men being saved.

> They are rich toward their own pleasures, or their own tastes, or their own families, but not rich toward God!
>
> They live as if they would not have to give an account of their use of money.
>
> They live as if there was no reckoning day before the bar of Christ.
>
> They live as if Christ had never said, "It is more blessed to give than to receive."

"Sell that ye have, and give alms. Provide yourselves bags which wax not old, a treasure in the heavens that faileth not."

Oh! If this book should by chance fall into the hands of such an one, I do beseech you, consider your ways and be wise. Cease to be content with giving God's cause a little.

- Give far more liberally than you have done yet.
- Give hundreds where you now give tens.
- Give thousands where you now give hundreds.

Then, and not till then, I shall believe you are "occupying" as one who looks for Christ's return. Alas! For the covetousness and narrow-mindedness of the Church of these days! May the Lord open the eyes of rich Christians.

Think again, how *instructive* are these words to all who are troubled by doubts about mingling with the world, and taking part in its vain amusements. It is useless to tell us that races, balls, and theaters, and operas, and cards, are not forbidden by name in Scripture. The question we should ask ourselves is simply this,—"Am I occupying as one who looks for Christ's return, when I take part in these things?

> Should I desire Jesus to return suddenly and find me at the race course, or in the ballroom, or at the theater, or at the card table?

Should I think I was in my right place, and where my Lord would have me to be?"

Oh, dear reader, this is the true test by which to try all our daily occupations and employments of time.

That thing which we would not do if we thought Jesus was coming tonight, that thing we ought not to do at all.

That place to which we would not go if we thought Jesus was coming this day, that place we ought to avoid.

That company in which we would not like Jesus to find us, in that company we ought never to sit down.

Oh, that men would live as in the sight of Christ! Not in the sight of man, or of the Church, or of ministers, —but as in the sight of Christ! This would be "occupying till He comes."

But think how *encouraging* are these words to all who seek first the kingdom of God, and love the Lord Christ in sincerity. What though the children of the world regard them as "righteous overmuch?" What though mistaken friends and relations tell them they pay too much attention to religion, and go too far! Those words, "Occupy till I come," are words which justify their conduct.

Let me conclude this address by a few words of general application.

1. WARNING

First let me draw from the whole subject a word of *solemn warning* for every one into whose hands this may fall. That warning is—that there is a great change yet to come on this world, and a change we ought to keep constantly before our mind's eye.

That change is *a change of masters*. That old rebel, the devil, and all his adherents, shall be cast down. The Lord Jesus arid all His saints shall be exalted and raised to honor. "The kingdoms of this world" shall "become the kingdoms of our Lord, and of His Christ."

That change is *a change of manners*. Sin shall no longer be made light of and palliated. Wickedness shall no longer go unpunished and unreproved. Holiness shall become the general character of the inhabitants of the earth. "The new heaven and the new earth" shall be the dwelling place of "righteousness."

That change *is a change of opinion*. There shall be no more deism, or skepticism, or infidelity. All nations shall do honor to the crucified Lamb of God. All men shall know Him, from the least to the greatest. "The earth shall be full of the knowledge of Him, as the waters cover the sea."

I say nothing as to the time when these things shall take place. I object, on principle, to all dogmatism about dates. All I insist upon is this—that there is a great change before us all; a change for the earth, a change for man, and, above all, a change for the saints. I accept the prediction that "There is a great improvement and development of human nature yet to take place." I accept it with all my heart. But how and when shall it be brought about? Not by any system of education. Not by any legislation of politicians. Not by anything short of the appearing of the kingdom of Christ. Then, and then only, shall there be universal justice, universal knowledge and universal peace.

I accept the common phrase of many, "There is a good time coming." I accept it with all my heart. I do verily believe there shall one day be no more poverty,—no more oppression,— no more ignorance, —no more grinding competition,—no more covetousness. But when shall that good time come? Never, never till the return of Jesus Christ at His second advent. And for whom shall that time be good? For none but those who know and love the Lord.

I accept the common phrase, "There is a man coming who will set all right, that is now wrong. We wait for the coming man." I accept it with all my heart. I do look for One who shall unravel the tangled skein of this world's affairs, and put everything in its right place. But who is the great physician for an old, diseased, worn-out world? It is the man Christ Jesus, who it yet to return.

Oh! Reader, let us realize this point. There is before us all a great change. Surely, when a man has notice to quit his present dwelling place, he ought to make sure that he has before him another home.

2. QUESTION

Next, let me draw from the whole subject a solemn question for all into whose hands this may fall. That question is simply this, ARE

YOU READY FOR THE GREAT CHANGE? Are you ready for the coming and kingdom of Christ?

Remember, I do not ask what you think about controversial points on the subject of prophecy. About all these points you and I may err, and yet be saved. The one point to which I want to hold you is this, "Are you ready for the kingdom of Christ?"

It is useless to tell me that in asking this, I put before you too high a standard. It is vain to tell me that a man may be a very good man, and yet not be ready for the kingdom of Christ. I deny it altogether. Every justified and converted man is ready, and if you are not ready, you are not a justified man.

The standard I put before you is nothing more than the New Testament standard, and the Apostles would have doubted the truth of your religion if you were not looking and longing for the coming of the Lord. Above all, the grand end of the Gospel is to prepare men to meet God. What has your Christianity done for you if it has not made you meet for the kingdom of Christ? Nothing! nothing, nothing at all! Oh, that you may think on this matter, and never rest till you are ready to meet Christ.

3. INVITATION

In the next place let me offer an invitation to all readers who do not feel ready for Christ's return. That invitation shall be short and simple. I beseech you to know your danger, and come to Christ without delay, that you may be pardoned, justified, and made ready for things to come.

I entreat you this day to "flee from the wrath to come," to the hope set before you in the Gospel. I pray you in Christ's stead, to lay down enmity and unbelief, and at once "to be reconciled to God."

Lay aside everything that stands between you and Christ. Cast away everything that draws you back, and prevents your feeling ready for the Lord's appearing. Find out the besetting sin that weighs you down, and tear it from your heart, however dear it may be. Cry mightily to the Lord Jesus to reveal Himself to your soul. Rest not till you have got a real, firm and reasonable hope, and know that your feet are on the Rock of Ages.

4. EXHORTATION

Last of all, let me draw from the subject an exhortation to all who know Christ indeed, and love His appearing. That exhortation is simply this,—that you strive more and more to be a "doing" Christian. Labor more and more to show forth the praises of Him who hath called you out of darkness into marvelous light. Improve every talent which the Lord Jesus has committed to your charge to the setting forth of His glory.

- Let your walk declare plainly that you seek a country yet to come.
- Let your conformity to the mind of Christ be unquestionable and unmistakable.
- Let your holiness be a clear plain fact, which even the worst enemies of the Gospel cannot deny.

Above all, if you are a student of prophecy, I entreat you never to let it be said that prophetical study prevents practical diligence.

- If you do believe that the day is really approaching, then labor actively to provoke others unto love and good works.
- If you do believe that the night is far spent, be doubly diligent to cast off the works of darkness and put on the armor of light.

Never was there a greater mistake than to fancy the doctrine of the personal return of Christ is calculated to paralyze Christian diligence. Surely there can be no greater spur to the servant's activity than the expectation of his master's speedy return.

This is the way to obtain a healthy state of soul. There is nothing like the exercises of our graces for promoting our spiritual vigor. Alas! there are not a few of God's saints who complain that they want spiritual comfort in their religion, while the fault is altogether in themselves. "OCCUPY," "OCCUPY,"

I would say to such persons. Lay yourselves out more heartily for the glory of God, and these uncomfortable feelings will soon vanish away. This is the way to do good to the children of the world.

Nothing, under God, has such an effect on unconverted people as the sight of a real, thorough going, live Christian. There are thousands who will not come to hear the Gospel, and do not know the meaning of justification by faith, who yet can understand an uncompromising, holy, consistent walk with God. "OCCUPY," "OCCUPY," I say again, if you want to do good.

> So living we shall find great joy in our work
> Great comfort in our trials
> Great doors of usefulness in the world
> Great consolation in our sickness
> Great hope in our death
> Leave great evidences behind us when we are buried
> Have great confidence in Christ's return
> Receive a great crown in the day of reward.

CHAPTER FOUR

THE SECOND COMING OF CHRIST

George Müller

Proved from Scripture—Not at Death—Coming Events—1. The First Resurrection—2. The Conversion and Restoration of Israel—3. Satan Bound—4. The Separation Between Wheat and Tares—5. The Destruction of Antichrist—Waiting for His Return—Watching—Working— Rewarded.

IN THE DAYS of the apostles the disciples were comforted and encouraged by the prospect of the personal return of the Lord Jesus Christ. An angel had said to them, as they watched the Lord depart from the earth, "Ye men of Galilee, why stand ye gazing up into heaven? This same Jesus, which is taken up from you into heaven, shall so come in like manner as ye have seen him go into heaven."

This was the hope of the Church; and thus it ought to have remained up to His actual return. His coming should have continued to be the hope of the Church; but this, alas! for centuries has not been the case.

In confessions of faith, the truth that the Lord Jesus will come again may still have a place; but practically, to by far the greater number of His disciples, it has been a mere doctrinal statement that has not been enjoyed, and which has had no influence upon their lives.

The Lord, however, desired it should be otherwise. He intended that His Church should look for Him; that she should watch and wait for His return. Again and again, during His personal ministry, the Lord Jesus foretold this great event; and after His ascension the apostle referred continually to it.

Very many passages of Scripture might be quoted in proof of this assertion, but I will only mention the following:

> "When the Son of man shall come in His glory, and all the holy angels with Him, then shall He sit upon the throne of His glory."

> "In my Father's house are many mansions; if it were not so I would have told you. I go to prepare a place for you. And if I go and prepare a place for you, I will come again and receive you unto myself; that where I am there ye may be also."

> "As it is appointed unto men once to die, and after this the judgment; so Christ was once offered to bear the sins of many; and unto them that look for Him shall He appear the second time, without sin unto salvation."

> "The Lord Himself shall descend from heaven with a shout."

These quotations suffice to prove that the second coming of the Lord Jesus means that He will return in person, and has no reference to the gift of the Holy Spirit on the day of Pentecost, or to His manifesting Himself in an especial manner to the believer in the way of comfort, instruction or help of any kind; nor has it reference to our death, when we, as believers, are taken to be with Him.

If, however, anyone should say, "Why lay such stress upon this; is not our going to Him when we die the same thing?" The reply is, "There is a vast difference between these two events."

NOT DEATH

(a) As *individuals* we shall at that time be brought only to a state of *partial* happiness; we shall have no glorified bodies then, but must await the hour when "in a moment, in the twinkling of an eye, at the last trump, the dead shall be raised incorruptible, and we shall be changed." Nor when we fall asleep do we reign with Christ and sit with Him upon His throne; because He will not then be manifestly reigning. Blessed therefore though it is for the child of God, when he departs "to be absent from the body and present with the Lord," it will be unspeakably more blessed still to enter upon that *fullness* of glory which awaits us only at our Lord's return.

(b) Satan will not be bound until Jesus comes again, and for this reason, by the permission of God, he still has power here, both in the world and in the Church, though individuals are out of his reach who have fallen asleep in Jesus.

(c) The whole Church will at once be introduced to full eternal happiness and glory at our blessed Lord's return. Not only as *individuals* will our cup of joy be full to overflowing, but we shall rejoice throughout eternity with the *whole company of the redeemed.*

COMING EVENTS

I now proceed to consider briefly some of the events which will take place then.

1. *The first resurrection,* when the changed and risen saints together will be caught up to meet the Lord in the air, to be forever with Him. At this time those only will be raised who, as believers in the Messiah under the old covenant dispensation, or as disciples of the Lord Jesus under that of the new covenant, shall have fallen asleep in Him.

The commonly received opinion is that at our Lord's return there will be a *general* resurrection, both of believers and unbelievers; while the Holy Spirit teaches in the Holy Scriptures that they who are Christ's, and they *only*, will have part in the first resurrection. In I Corinthians we read thus: "As in Adam all die, even so in Christ shall all be made alive. But every man in his own order; Christ the first fruits, afterward *they that are Christ's* at His coming."

Notice the words, "they that are *Christ's*." Not *all* who had previously died, but those only who through faith in Jesus are united to Him, and shall have fallen asleep as believers. The same truth is taught in I Thessalonians, where we read: "The *dead in Christ* shall rise first. Then (afterward) we which are alive and remain shall be caught up together with them in the clouds to meet the Lord in the air; and so shall we ever be with the Lord." Notice that only of the dead in Christ it is said they will rise at that time.

> "And I saw a great white throne, and Him that sat on it, from whose face the earth and the heaven fled away; and there was found no place for them. And I saw the dead, small and great, stand before God; and the books were opened; and another book was opened, which is the book of life; and the dead were judged out of those things which were written in the books, according to their works. And the sea gave up the dead which were in it; and death and hell delivered up the dead which were in them; and they were judged every man according to their works. And death and hell were cast into the lake of fire. This is the second death. And whosoever was not found written in the book of life was cast into the lake of fire."

Oh! how should the *solemnity* and *certainty* of these events come home to every one of us, and with what earnestness should each person who reads these lines seek upon scriptural grounds to settle for himself that he is really Christ's. By nature we are lost, ruined and undone, and deserve nothing but punishment; but we have, at the same time, to accept God's only remedy, namely, salvation through faith in the blood and righteousness of the Lord Jesus Christ, by whom alone spiritual life, pardon and justification can be obtained.

2. *The conversion and restoration of Israel nationally*. In Scripture the glory and resurrection of the Church of the firstborn ones is always connected with the time when Israel (who will have returned to their own land in unbelief) "shall know the Lord."

3. Another event which will take place at the return of the Lord Jesus, is that *Satan will be bound*.

> "And I saw an angel come down from heaven, having the key of the bottomless pit and a great chain in his hand. And he laid hold on the dragon, that old serpent, which is the devil and Satan, and bound him a thousand years, and cast him into the bottomless pit, and shut him up and set a seal upon him, that he should deceive the nations no more till the thousand years should be fulfilled, and after that he must be loosed a little season."

During the present dispensation, *before* the return of our Lord, Satan will not be bound; therefore sin and open wickedness will continue to the end of it, and instead of becoming better, things, according to Scripture, will become worse and worse. It is impossible to shut one's eyes to the fearful wickedness now around us everywhere. Murders of the most cruel character, and numerous other atrocious crimes are, even in this enlightened nineteenth century, continually being committed.

How certainly does all this prove that Satan is not yet bound, that he is even now the god of this world, and has power still; and because he knows that his time will be comparatively short, he manifests his hatred against God and against His people to the very utmost.

But this state of things will not always last, for when Jesus comes again he will lose his power in the earth, and will be shut up in the bottomless pit for a thousand years.

4. In connection with the return of the Lord Jesus is another event, namely, the *separation between the wheat and the tares,* which represent Christendom, or the professing Church of Christ. Read carefully Matthew, thirteen, verses thirty-seven to forty:

> "He that soweth the good seed is the Son of man; the field is the world; the good seed are the children of the kingdom; but the tares are the children of the wicked one; the enemy that sowed them is the devil; the harvest is the end of the world; and the reapers are the angels. As therefore the tares are gathered and burned in the fire, so shall it be in the end of this world."

In this parable, together with our Lord's own explanation of it, we see what is to be expected during this present dispensation, while Jesus tarries. Civilization, mental cultivation, and advancement in knowledge of every kind, may continue to the utmost; but man, fallen man, remains a ruined creature, except he be regenerated by the power of the Holy Spirit, through the acceptance of the Gospel. Intellectually he may be improved and polished to the very highest degree, but he is a sinner, and, in his natural condition, remains lost, ruined and undone. He may even possess natural religion and a form of godliness, but if he is not born again he is still at enmity with God, and as assuredly as he does not believe in the Lord Jesus Christ, "the wrath of God abideth on him."

Sin is not, as some suppose, a *comparatively little thing*. It is a deadly spiritual disease, as the Word of God declares it to be; and

The Second Coming Of Christ

no progress in education, no mental culture, can eradicate it from the heart, or change depraved human nature. Notwithstanding every effort at improvement, the heart remains "deceitful above all things and desperately wicked." Until the return of the Lord Jesus, therefore, the present state of things will continue, and, as we shall see presently from the Word of God, will become worse and worse.

This, then, plainly shows the notion entertained by many godly, excellent persons, that the world will be converted during the present dispensation by the preaching of the Gospel, and that the millennium will thus finally be introduced, to be not according to the Holy Scriptures.

The Gospel, indeed, is to be preached *"as a witness* to all nations," but it is not to be the means of the *conversion* of the world. Moreover, we learn the character of the present dispensation, which is, that God *takes out* from among the Gentiles a people for His name, but does not *convert* all nations.

This is confirmed by the parable of the wheat and the tares; for if the whole world were to be converted before the return of the Lord Jesus, there would be no truth in the explanation given of it by our Lord Himself.

He tells us that the tares (the children of the wicked one) were to grow together with the wheat (the children of the kingdom), until the end of the age, namely up to the time of His own return. This, therefore, the Word of the Lord Jesus, is in direct opposition to the common notion that the world will be converted previous to His coming again.

And in addition to this, we find passage after passage in the New Testament in which we are expressly told either by Christ or by the apostles, that at the close of the present dispensation wickedness will abound both among professed believers and in the world at large, in proof of which I will refer to one single passage of Scripture only.

We read in another place:

> "This know also, that in the last days perilous times shall come. For men shall be lovers of their own selves, covetous, boasters, proud, blasphemers, disobedient to parents, unthankful, unholy, without nat-

ural affection, truce-breakers, false accusers, inconsistent, fierce, despisers of those that are good, traitors, heady, high-minded, lovers of pleasure more than lovers of God; having a *form of godliness* but denying the power thereof."

Here we have particularly to keep before us that this is not a description of pagans, but of the professed disciples of the Lord Jesus; for to such a state will Christendom, or the professing Church of Christ, be reduced at the end of the present dispensation.

Notice especially that of these persons it is said, they have a *form* of godliness. They wish to be considered Christians. They are not avowed infidels and atheists, but professed believers. Are we, then, to expect that things around us will gradually improve, or rather, that, as we approach

THE END OF THE AGE

the darker they will become? True it is that one day, "The earth will be filled with the knowledge of the Lord, as the waters cover the sea," but this will never be until Jesus Himself comes. In the meantime lawlessness will increase, and the socialism, the communism, the nihilism, etc., of which we now hear so much, will at last be headed up in the personal Antichrist, the man of sin.

This leads me to mention another of the events that will take place at the return of the Lord Jesus, namely:

5. *The destruction of the Antichrist.*

"Now we beseech you brethren, by (or, concerning) the coming of our Lord Jesus Christ, and by (or, concerning) our gathering together unto Him, that ye be not soon (or, hastily) shaken in mind or be troubled, neither by spirit nor by word nor by letter as from us, as that (or, as though he had said) the day of Christ is at hand.

Let no man deceive you by any means, for that day shall not come except there come a falling away (or the apostasy) first, and that (or the) man of sin be revealed, the son of perdition; who opposeth and exalteth himself above all that is called God and that is worshiped: that he as God sitteth in the temple of God, showing himself that he is God. Remember ye not that when I was yet with you I told you of these things.

"And now ye know what withholdeth that he might be revealed in his time. For the mystery of iniquity (or lawlessness) doth already work, only he who now letteth (or, restraineth) will let, until he be taken out of the way. And then shall that wicked (or, lawless one) be revealed, whom the Lord shall consume with the spirit of His mouth and destroy with the brightness of His coming."

We have now in the next place to consider that it is the will of the Lord that we, His disciples, should

WAIT FOR HIS RETURN.

A great many passages might be quoted from the New Testament in proof of this; but for the sake of brevity, I will refer only to a few. In Titus, we read,

"The grace of God that bringeth salvation hath appeared to all men, teaching us that denying ungodliness and worldly lusts, we should live soberly, righteously and godly in this present world. Looking for that blessed hope and the glorious appearing of the great God and our Savior Jesus Christ."

Observe how it is laid upon the saints to look for the blissful hope and the appearing of the glory of the great God and our Savior Jesus Christ.

WATCH

The Lord said to His disciples, "*Watch* therefore, for ye know neither the day nor the hour when the Son of man cometh."

Again He said, "Watch ye therefore, for ye know not when the master of the house cometh, at even, or at midnight, or at the cock crowing, or in the morning; lest coming suddenly, he find you sleeping. And what I say unto you, I say unto all, Watch."

Again, the Lord says, "Behold I come as a thief. Blessed is he that watcheth, and keepeth his garments, lest he walk naked and they see his shame."

Now, are we, as believers, all watching? are we earnestly longing for the return of that blessed One? Do our hearts truly yearn after Him, and long for His glorious appearing? Are we also doing our part to hasten on His coming? And is it habitually our prayer that the Lord will be pleased to hasten the fulfillment of events yet to be fulfilled before that day comes?

PRACTICAL EFFECTS

And now the last part of our subject remains to be considered, namely, the practical effect this truth should have upon our hearts. If it be really received and entered into, the child of God will say, "What can I do for my blessed Savior before He comes again? How can I most glorify Him? His will concerning me is that I should occupy 'until He come.' How then can I best use for Him the talents with which I am entrusted, by physical strength, my mental powers? How can my sight, my tongue, all my faculties of mind and body, be best devoted to His praise? How should my time, my money, all that I am and have, be used for Him? How can my whole spirit, soul and body be best consecrated to His service?"

These are deeply important practical questions which all believers in the Lord Jesus should ask themselves seeing that we are not our own, but are bought with a price, even with His precious blood. Instead of indulging in inactivity and listlessness on account of the evil state of things around us, we should pray and work, and work and pray, as if it were in our power to stem the torrent of abounding iniquity.

Who can say how much good one single child of God, who is thoroughly in earnest, may accomplish, and how greatly he may glorify God by walking in entire separation from all that is hateful to Him? We have especially also to guard against the temptation of slackening our efforts for the conversion of sinners, because the world will not be converted before Jesus comes.

Rather should we say, "The time that He delayeth His coming may be short: what therefore can I do to warn sinners, and to win souls for Him?"

In conclusion, I would direct attention to II Peter, third chapter, verses eleven to fourteen:

> "Seeing then that all these things shall be dissolved, what manner of persons ought we to be in holy conversation and godliness, looking for and hasting unto the coming (or hastening the coming) of the day of God, wherein the heavens being on fire shall be dissolved, and the elements shall melt with fervent heat? Nevertheless, we, according to His promise, look for new heavens and a new earth wherein dwelleth

righteousness. Wherefore, beloved, seeing that ye look for such things, be diligent, that ye may be found of Him in peace, without spot and blameless."

As assuredly as the practical character of the Lord's second coming is really apprehended in the power of it, the most blessed effects upon the life and deportment of Christians will follow.

By means of it we are taught what awaits the world lying in the wicked one, and what will be the end of the world's glory, pride and pomp. The future destiny of the children of God is also unfolded to us, even that we shall be perfectly conformed to the image of our risen Lord, both in soul and body, when we shall see Him as He is.

Then shall we enter upon the possession of our inheritance which is incorruptible and undefiled, and that fadeth not away; and we shall be seated with Jesus on His throne, to judge the world in union with Him, and to spend a happy eternity together with our Lord in glory. "Behold I come quickly, and my reward is with me, to give every man according as his work shall be."

CHAPTER FIVE

THE SECOND COMING OF OUR LORD

D. W. Whittle

The Practical Bearing of the Doctrine—Seven Cardinal Points—1. Not Death—2. Not the Destruction of Jerusalem—3. Not the Coming of the Holy Spirit—4. Personal and Visible—5. Its Aspect to Israel—6. To the Unbelieving World—7. And to the Church

THE ONLY PEOPLE I have ever found in this country or any other country who show that they have really been stimulated to Christian work, are those who have first got *the truth* into their hearts; and there is no truth, according to my observation, that has so stimulated men to consecration and work for Christ as the truth of the Scriptures concerning the personal coming of the Lord Jesus.

There is nothing that has so blessed me as to see this truth. Nothing did so much to get me into Christian work. Evangelists throughout the country, as a rule, hold the truth as to the second coming of the Lord and are blessed by it. And when you see ministers from the Atlantic to the Pacific coast that are being blessed and filled with the Spirit, and people love to hear the Word of God from them, you will usually find that this truth has been opened up to them. Then let us dismiss our prejudices. Let us look to the Holy Ghost to be our Teacher.

There is nothing in this truth that is so very mysterious. It is just as plain and simple as can be when you take a common-sense presentation of it. What we want is to take the Bible as it reads—to let the Word of God speak to us just as God has given it, and lay aside all preconceived ideas and notions, and the vagaries of men. The doctrine has been shamefully abused. Dates have been set, ascension robes prepared, and fanatical teachings spread abroad.

Hence there has been a great reaction. But all this is the work of the devil. He wants to get God's people away from the truth. Yet the truth is in the Scriptures, and we will find it there if we look for it.

Now there are seven points that I want to make clear in connection with this doctrine:

I

First, *the coming of the Lord mentioned in the Scriptures is not death*. "If I will that he tarry till I come, what is that to thee?" The disciples had an idea that John was not to die, but that he was to tarry on the earth until the Lord Jesus should come again. They did not understand that the coming of the Lord meant death.

Again: "Behold, I show you a mystery. We shall not all sleep, but we shall all be changed." That is, we shall not all die, but we shall all be changed when the Lord comes.

Again, Paul says: "For I am in a strait betwixt two, having a desire to depart, and to be with Christ, which is far better." That was his idea of what dying was—not the coming of the Lord to him, but his departing to be with the Lord. Dying is departing to be with the Lord, and the coming of the Lord mentioned in the Scriptures is the Lord coming to this earth for us.

John says: "Then said Jesus unto them plainly, Lazarus is dead. And I am glad for your sakes that I was not there, to the extent that ye might believe; nevertheless, let us go unto him." That is: "He is in the grave. I am going to raise him from the dead; and in his resurrection I am to be glorified, and you will understand My power as you never did before." That is where the resurrection came in—God was to be glorified in the resurrection.

Now, Jesus was on His way to Lazarus. Was the death of Lazarus the coming of Christ? Jesus said: "Let us go to him." What for? To raise him from the dead. Then the coming of Christ was not his death, but the very opposite.

I suppose if some of those brethren had been there who explain away the Scriptures by saying that the coming of the Lord means death, and if they had been called upon to preach the funeral sermon, they would have said:

> "Dear friends— We know very well that Jesus promised Mary and Martha that He would come and we know very well that He is on His way. We believe He will fulfill His word. But don't you see, dear friends, that this is the meaning of His words: Lazarus is dead, and the Lord has come. He has come in death. That is how He has fulfilled His word."

Still, that wasn't the fulfillment of it at all. Lazarus' death meant an entirely different thing, and the coming of the Lord meant resurrection. It doesn't mean death; it means life.

II

The second point I would make is this: *The coming of the Lord is not the destruction of Jerusalem.*

> "When ye shall see Jerusalem compassed with armies, then know that the desolation thereof is nigh. Then let them which are in Judea flee to the mountains . . . And Jerusalem shall be trodden down of the Gentiles, until the times of the Gentiles be fulfilled."

The fulfillment of this prophecy is still going on evidently. Jerusalem is still trodden under foot of the Gentiles.

In this passage there are two things spoken of: first, the destruction of Jerusalem; and then a judgment coming upon corrupt Christendom. I think the destruction of Jerusalem is a type of that which will come upon corrupt Christendom when the times of the Gentiles are fulfilled. Judaism became corrupt.

When Christ came, the people as a whole would not receive Him. And there were Sadducees denying the resurrection. But there was a little company of Jews that were godly—righteous Pharisees, awaiting the coming of the Messiah. The religion of the nation, as a nation, was corrupt. What is Christendom today? We forget that true believers are a mere handful as compared with the great mass that profess the name of Jesus Christ. In the time of our Lord's ministry the prominent thing in the minds of the disciples was Judaism—the Temple, and all the ritualism of the Jewish religion—and in this passage the first thing Christ said was: *"This is all to be swept away. Your Temple is to be destroyed.*" Then beyond that He told them of further events pertaining to the latter day.

> "Behold, He cometh with clouds; and every eye shall see Him, and they also which pierceth Him: and all countries of the earth shall wail because of Him. Even so, Amen."

This is in the last book of the Bible. The book of Revelation was written according to our chronology, nearly the year 96. It was written by John when he was an old man. John wrote his Epistles in the year 90, and the book of Revelation a few years later. And this last book of the inspired volume is full of testimony concerning the second coming of our Lord. Well, Jerusalem was destroyed in the year 70. Consequently Jerusalem was destroyed many years before John wrote the book of Revelation. In the writing of Revelation the time of the coming of the Lord was still future.

When any one asks you on this point you can just say: "How is it that John, after Jerusalem was destroyed, still bears testimony to the coming of the Lord as a future event?"

III

The third point is that *the coming of the Lord is not the coming of the Holy Spirit*. "It is expedient for you that I go away, for if I go not away the Comforter will not come unto you; but if I depart I will send Him unto you." "But ye shall receive power, after that the Holy Ghost is come upon you." "And they were all filled with the Holy Ghost, and began to speak with other tongues as the Spirit gave them utterance."

The Holy Spirit came on the day of Pentecost. Then, according to the argument that the coming referred to was the coming of the Spirit, after the Spirit has come you will not hear anything more of the coming of Christ. But how is it? After the Holy Ghost came, you hear a great deal more about the coming of Christ than ever before. Again: "He shall send Jesus Christ . . . whom the heaven must receive until the times of restitution of all things." Peter was filled with the Holy Ghost while delivering this sermon, and his testimony is to direct the people to the fact that Jesus is coming back to this earth. In view of that he says: "Repent, and be converted, that your sins may be blotted out when the times of refreshing shall come from the presence of the Lord."

IV

The fourth point is that *the coming of Christ is a personal and visible coming,*

> "And as they thus spake, Jesus Himself stood in the midst of them, and said unto them, Peace be unto you Behold My hands and My feet, that it is I Myself: handle Me, and see; for a spirit hath not flesh and bones, as ye see Me have And they gave Him a piece of broiled fish, and of an honeycomb. And He took it, and did eat before them."

It was the person of our risen Lord; not a vision—not an intangible something or other. A real living person stood before them. "

> To whom also He showed Himself alive after His passion by many infallible proofs . . . When He had spoken these things, while they beheld, He was taken up; and a cloud received Him out of their sight This same Jesus, who is taken up from you into heaven, shall so come in like manner as ye have seen him go into heaven."

Could anything be more real than that?

Thank God for facts! Thank God that we have a Gospel based on facts. It is a fact that I am a sinner—that you are a sinner; a hell-deserving sinner condemned by God's law. It is a fact that you need a Savior. It is a fact that Christ was born of the Virgin Mary, lived on this earth, obeyed the law, was crucified under Pontius Pilate; that His literal body rose again, and that that literal body ascended into Heaven.

And it is a fact that angels convoyed Him, and said: "This same Jesus . . . shall so come in like manner as ye have seen him go into Heaven." Let us believe. Let us take the Word of God as God has given it to us, and we cannot go astray.

"He fell to the earth, and heard a voice saying unto him, Saul, Saul, why persecutest thou Me? And he said, Who art thou, Lord? And the Lord said, I am Jesus whom thou persecutest." It was no vision. Paul saw Jesus Christ, and the men that were with him heard a voice. It was the Lord in His personality. "After that, He was seen of five hundred brethren at once . . . And last of all He was seen of me also, as of one born out of due time."

On the way to Damascus Paul was placed among the witnesses to Jesus Christ. He saw Him, had an interview with Him—personal and visible. Well, now; if the Lord could come back and be personal and visible on that road to Damascus, cannot He come back again, and be personal and visible on this earth when it shall please Him to do so? "If I go and prepare a place for you, I will come again, and receive you unto Myself, that where I am, there ye may be also." "I go"; "I come." He went away in person and He says, "I will come again." It is the same "I" that comes. "If I go, I come." "For the Lord *Himself* shall descend with a shout." "The Lord Himself." How blessed, and how comforting!

When an old woman was dying, someone said that the angels would soon come for her.

"Oh, no," said she; "the Lord Himself will come."

There is no other comfort for one who is truly born of God. It is the Lord Himself, who was here —personal and visible—that is coming to take His saints to Himself.

V

The fifth heading. There are three things connected with His coming, and it has helped me to view it in three aspects. We must rightly divide the Word of God. The man that has only one pigeon-hole, and puts into it everything in the Word of God, is likely to get things badly mixed up. The Holy Ghost has given us three pigeon-holes—Jew, Gentile, and the Church of God. One portion of the Word of God is for one, another for the second, and another for the third. I want, under this fifth heading, to consider the *coming of our Lord in its aspect to Israel*.

> "O Jerusalem, Jerusalem, thou that killest the prophets . . . ye shall not see Me henceforth, till ye shall say, Blessed is He that cometh in the name of the Lord."

There is the final farewell of Israel's Messiah to Israel. He withdraws, and shortly after is crucified, and now He is being preached to the Gentiles. Again: "For if the casting away of them be the reconciling of the world, what shall the receiving of them be, but life from the dead?" Also: "For I would not, brethren, that ye should be ignorant of this mystery." How many of us are ignorant? Seven times this phrase is used in the New Testament. There are seven things the Holy Ghost doesn't want Christians to be ignorant of. Let us hear what this one is:

"Blindness in part is happened to Israel, until the fullness of the Gentiles be come in. And so all Israel shall be saved: as it is written, There shall come out of Zion the Deliverer . . . As touching the election they are beloved for the fathers' sakes."

Yes; though you may despise them, they are beloved. Every Jew is an object of God's special love. He may be down in Chatham Street, selling old trousers, or old army-blankets dyed and scoured, or old slouch hats. You may despise the Jews', but they are beloved for the fathers' sakes. They are the seed of Abraham, and they are dear to the Lord Jesus Christ. Paul was ready to die that they might have the light of the Gospel.

> "In that day shall the Lord defend the inhabitants of Jerusalem . . .
> And the Lord shall be king over all the earth: in that day there shall be one Lord, and His name One."

These words are just as plain as they can be, if people will only read them, and believe them as they read. Don't take any commentator and let him explain away the plain sense.

John Bunyan was once studying this passage, and when he came to the words foretelling that the feet of the Lord should stand on the Mount of Olives, he thus reasoned: *"Some commentators say that the Mount of Olives means the heart of the believer, that it is only a figurative expression, and means that the Lord will reign in the heart of the believer, and the Holy Ghost will dwell there. But I don't think it means that at all. I just think it means the Mount of Olives, two miles from Jerusalem, on the east."*

Look at poor Israel today. How literally God's Word regarding them is being fulfilled. They are scattered among all nations. Down in New Orleans, in a Hebrew cemetery, you will see this inscription in Hebrew letters over the roadway: "The dispersed of Judah." I pity any believing man that isn't touched by that. At that day, when Christ shall come—oh, what a revelation to Israel! Jerusalem shall be rebuilt, and Christ their Messiah recognized.

They will say, "What are these wounds in thine hands?"—and He will say, "I was wounded in the house of My friends"; and they will bow down before Him and acknowledge Him as King. This aspect of the coming of the Lord fulfills every promise made to Abraham, Isaac Jacob and David.

VI

The sixth point is the *aspect of the coming of the Lord to the unbelieving world.*

> "And after they had held their peace, James answered, saying, Men and brethren, hearken unto me. Simon hath declared how God at the first did visit the Gentiles, to take out of them a people for His name."

That is the present dispensation. There is nothing said about the conversion of the world. But God is now visiting the Gentiles to take out of them a people for His name. "To this agree the words of the prophets; as it is written, After this I will return, and will build again the tabernacle of David, which is fallen down."

"Fallen down"—what does that mean? Read the whole prophecy from which it is taken, and find a description of Israel. "I will build again the ruins thereof, and I will set it up: that the residue of men might seek after the Lord, and all the Gentiles upon whom my name is called."

After the tabernacle of David is rebuilt, and the promises to Israel are fulfilled, what then, the destruction of the world? No; there is to be an opportunity for the residue of men to seek after the Lord, and all the Gentiles shall learn of Him. "The earth shall be filled with the knowledge of the glory of the Lord as the waters cover the sea."

Will there be a judgment? Yes—for the impenitent ones, the ungodly ones, those that have rejected Christ.

Will there be a destruction of the world? No; there is to be a glorious time on this earth.

> "The Lord Jesus shall be revealed from heaven with His mighty angels, in flaming fire taking vengeance upon them that know not God, and that obey not the Gospel of our Lord Jesus Christ; who shall be punished with everlasting destruction from the presence of the Lord, and from the glory of His power."

There is the judgment of those that have rejected the Gospel. They are in danger today. I do not like to put a thousand years between us and the judgment of the wicked. I believe it is an awful error to do so. The impenitent are in danger this very hour, and we are not warning them as we should. I don't see a shadow of hope for those who have heard the Gospel and had Gospel privileges and up to this time are rejecting Christ. The judgment is for them—then punishment is for them.

See Zechariah: *"Every one that is left of all the nations which came against Jerusalem, shall go up from year to year to worship the King, the Lord of hosts, and to keep the feast of tabernacles."* At the appearing of the Lord to set up His kingdom the world is not destroyed, evidently. There are nations left to go up.

> "I saw the souls of them that were beheaded for the witness of Jesus, . . . and they lived and reigned with Christ a thousand years. And the rest of the dead lived not again until the thousand years were finished. This is the first resurrection. Blessed and holy is he that hath part in the first resurrection; on such the second death hath no power, but they shall be priests of God, and shall reign with Him a thousand years."

Here is where we get the millennium. Now you see the meaning of the word "premillennial." "Pre" means "before." The premillennial advent means Christ coming before the millennium.

There will be no millennium till He comes. That is plain Scripture. Many people have an idea that we are going to get the millennium by means of telephones, steam engines, swift Atlantic steamers, and all the appliances of modern civilization. These things, they imagine, are to bring the millennium, and then at the end of the millennium Christ will come.

But it is Scripture that Christ will come first. He must come before His reign of a thousand years. He is to usher in the millennium by His coming. If the postmillennial theory is true, when is the millennium to commence? Certainly it hasn't come yet, nor does it seem to be coming. Look at London, with its millions in degradation and sin. Look at our own country, and its great cities like Chicago, with Anarchists and Communists propagating their doctrines.

If the world is to become better first, we are very far from the millennium yet. But death is here; sin is here.

Telephones and swift steamships don't change the heart. We may have a wonderful civilization, but that is not regeneration.

The time described in Scriptures has not begun to dawn yet. But it is coming. It is not for us to know the times and seasons; but when it comes it will not be by means of modern inventions and discoveries. The Lord Jesus Christ will get the victory, and *He* will get the glory.

VII

And now, what is *the aspect of the coming of the Lord to His Church? This is my seventh point.*

> "He said unto His disciples, The days will come, when ye shall desire to see one of the days of the Son of Man, and ye shall not see it. And they shall say to you, See here! or, See there!
>
> Go not after them, nor follow them. For as the lightning that lighteneth out of the one part under heaven, shineth unto the other part under heaven, so shall also the Son of Man be in His day."

That is the warning for us. Some years ago in Jerusalem there was a man who said he was the Lord, and people followed after him. In Cincinnati there was a woman who believed she was the Lord. Christ warns us that there will be people saying "Lo here!" and "Lo, there!" There will be delusions. Don't be occupied with them. The Lord doesn't give us any dates, but He just tells us to watch.

When He comes there will be no deception; it will be plain to us all. It will be like the lightning shining throughout the whole sky. Don't be carried away by those who fix dates and are occupied with delusions. "It is not for you to know the times and the seasons which the Father hath put in His own power." Let us rest there, living in an attitude of expectation— living in a spirit of consecration—doing God's work faithfully, so that we are ready to meet Him if He should come today.

> "Take heed unto yourselves, lest at any time your hearts be overcharged with surfeiting and drunkenness, and cares of this Me, and so

that day come upon you unawares. For as a snare shall it come upon all them that dwell on the face of the whole earth. Watch ye, therefore, and pray always, that ye may be accounted worthy to escape all these things that shall come to pass, and to stand before the Son of Man."

That is where some of us feel that we have our hope of the rapture of the Church. Some people think we are going to be put through tribulations-going to be sifted and tested. I think the Lord will give us discipline before His appearing. But if we are watching and ready, we shall be "accounted worthy to escape all these things."

See I Thessalonians: "We which are alive and remain shall be caught up together with them in the clouds, to meet the Lord in the air; and so shall we ever be with the Lord. Wherefore comfort one another with these words."

And thank God for their inexpressible comfort: "The dead in Christ shall rise first!"

You have loved ones laid away in the cemetery. Their bodies are resting—waiting for the resurrection. At the voice of the archangel they shall rise and receive their new bodies. They have followed Jesus in going down into the grave, and they shall have their precedence—or shall have their glorified bodies before us who may be living. But immediately we shall be caught up with them to meet the Lord in the air, "and so shall we ever be with the Lord."

We are certainly associated with them in His glory. When He sets up His kingdom on earth, His Bride will be with Him. Where shall I be? I shall be with Christ, together with all the saints, and we shall judge the earth. When Christ comes we shall be associated with Him in His reign.

Therefore, dear friends, the aspect to us of Christ's appearing involves:

(1). Deliverance from this present evil world. "Who gave Himself for our sins, that He might deliver us from this present evil world, according to the will of God and our Father."

(2). Deliverance from judgment. "And to wait for His Son from heaven, whom He raised from the dead, even Jesus which delivered us from the wrath to come."

(3). Deliverance from this body of corruption. "The creature itself shall also be delivered from the bondage of corruption into the glorious liberty of the children of God Even we ourselves groan within ourselves, waiting for the adoption, to wit the redemption of our body."

(4). Gathering with loved ones. Many of our families have been scattered; the dear ones are far away; but when Christ comes there will be a great home gathering.

(5). Our seeing Jesus. "Beloved, now are we the sons of God; and it doth not yet appear what we shall be: but we know that, when He shall appear, we shall be like Him; for we shall see Him as He is."

I like the thought that our union with Christ is a real union. Everything that concerns me. Christ is concerned in; and everything that concerns Christ, I am concerned in. So it is in regard to this coming of Christ, in regard to the setting up of His kingdom on earth, and in regard to the manifestation of His glory.

Oh, how selfish and vain, how narrow is the range of that man's vision who can only think of these things in connection with his miserable self! These concern the glory of the Lord Jesus Christ. At the Mount of Olives, where they put the mock scepter in His hand, and spat upon Him, and derided Him—in that very place Jesus Christ is to come and be made manifest in His glory. It is all His glory. You poor, miserable, selfish man or woman, do you think that Christ died simply to keep you out of Hell—simply to make you happy?

The Bible tells you from beginning to end that your salvation is not your own salvation merely, but that Jesus Christ may be glorified. Your pardon shows His grace; your sanctification shows His holiness; your resurrection shows His power; and your being glorified is to reflect His glory. It all concerns Him, and because it concerns Him it ought to concern us; and we ought to love—oh!

How we ought to love!—His glorious appearing.

CHAPTER SIX

THE BLESSED HOPE

George C. Needham

It is Purifying—Pacifying—Comforting—Glorious—Promised Glories—What Should be our Present Attitude?

WHATEVER MEANING we may put on the prophetic event introduced in the Scriptures as our Lord's second coming, we must observe that it is frequently specified as A HOPE. And as hope implies expectation, the conviction of something unfulfilled, that term alone designates the Advent as a future thing.

Hope is the opposite of despair. It has a definite object in view, and as that object is apprehended at hand or remotely, the soul is swayed by delight or discouragement. The blessed hope and coming in glory of our Lord Jesus Christ should not be relegated to the regions of mystery.

How can it be a hope of any value if it be some uncertain, indefinite, faraway, and nonessential theory which happened to drop into the Bible? In fifty-three places where hope is referred to in the divine Word, it has special relation to future blessings which are to crown the Christian believer at the appearing of Jesus Christ. A few of these we might examine:

1. IT IS A BLESSED HOPE

"Looking for the blessed hope and appearing of the glory of our great God and Savior Jesus Christ."

A blessed hope means a happy one. The word refers to inward enjoyment apart from external environment. The expectations implied in such a hope make all present circumstances of trial or depression "not worthy to be compared with the glory which shall be revealed to usward.

For the earnest expectation of the creation waiteth for the manifestation of the sons of God."

2. IT IS A PURIFYING HOPE

"And every man that hath this hope in him purifieth himself, even as he is pure."

As linen bleaches under the sun, the light of this hope cleanses the life from the world-stains. It loosens the grasp from the things of earth. The man who has a magnificent mansion in some beautiful locality, and is only tarrying in a city hotel for a few days till he can journey home, will not care to spend his time and money in elaborately decorating his temporary lodging in the strange city.

If he purchases bric-a-brac or pictures, the though in his mind is, "I will take them home." So the Christian, who reckons himself a "pilgrim and a stranger" here, will have little heart to spend his energies on things pertaining merely to the earthly His city and his home lie beyond. His great concern will be to lay up treasures in heaven."

3. IT IS A PACIFYING HOPE

> "Therefore judge nothing before the time, until the Lord come, who will both bring to light the hidden things of darkness, and will make manifest the counsels of the hearts; and then shall every man have praise of God." "Be patient, therefore, brethren, unto the coming of the Lord. Behold, the husbandman waiteth for the precious fruit of the earth, and hath long patience for it, until he receive the early and the latter rain. Be ye also patient; stablish your hearts; for the coming of the Lord draweth nigh."

In the power of this hope all questions of provocation can be patiently laid aside for the Lord to settle on His arrival. The child of God who is pervaded with this hope will be willing to waive all rights of self-vindication, knowing that his "labor of love and patience of hope" will not go unrewarded.

4. IT IS A COMFORTING HOPE

> "But I would not have you to be ignorant, brethren, concerning them which are asleep, that ye sorrow not even as others which have no hope."

The luster of this hope shines most conspicuously in the consolation it brings to those who are called to part with their loved ones by death. The unbelieving bury their dead without any certain or definite expectation of reunion. For in no human scheme of philosophy is the truth of a resurrection even hinted at.

But the Scriptures definitely promise this. "For if we believe that Jesus died and rose again, even them also which sleep in Jesus will God bring with Him."

The Apostle Paul, after explaining all this to the Thessalonian Christians, and showing them the immense advantage they had over the heathen who knew nothing about the advent majesty of Jesus Christ, or of the resurrection, add finally, "Wherefore comfort one another with these words."

5. IT IS A GLORIOUS HOPE

> "For our citizenship is in heaven; from whence also we wait for a Savior, the Lord Jesus Christ; who shall fashion anew the body of our humiliation that it may be conformed to the body of his glory according to the working whereby he is able even to subject all things unto himself."

> "By faith Abraham, when he was tried, offered up Isaac; and he that received the promises offered up his only begotten son, of whom it was said, that in Isaac shall thy seed be called; accounting that God was able to raise him up, even from the dead; from whence also he received him in a figure . . . Women received their dead raised to life again; and others were tortured, not accepting deliverance; that they might obtain a better resurrection."

This hope would be meaningless apart from the locality and the circumstances where it anchors itself. It leaps over time and space to the period when Jesus Christ shall Himself be glorified as King of kings according to the eternal purpose of the Father.

PROMISES

This blessed hope embraces several promised glories:

1. *We shall be with Christ*. Not as in death, when we are said to be "unclothed" and "waiting to be clothed upon with our house from heaven." In an actual sense we shall "see Him as He is," and be ourselves like Him, personally and morally.

2. *We shall be beyond sinning*. Now we groan for deliverance. Pain and the curse encompass us.

The consummation of that hope will bring full redemption to the body.

3. *We shall know as we are known*. "Now we see through a glass darkly, but then face to face; now I know in part; but then shall I know even as also I am known."

What joy to have the hope of one day being masters of all knowledge; to understand the mysteries of science, the marvels of astronomy, the secrets of nature, and the profound depths of the soul!

WHAT SHOULD BE OUR PRESENT ATTITUDE?

We ought to be *looking* for the blessed crisis. That is, expecting it with desire. We should be praying for it and thereby seek to hasten it. We should anticipate its consummation by our endeavor of personal faithfulness toward all that it involves. We ought to be loving it.

If we love the seed of Abraham, if we love the burdened brute creation, if we love the heathen Gentile nations who know nothing of a Savior, we shall joyfully welcome this hope, for their sakes also. For it is the hope that shall I bring to the Jew his Messiah; to the creature his emancipation from man's exacting dominion; to mute nature her freedom from thorns and thistles; to the heathen idolater a knowledge of the true and' living God; and to the waiting Bride the personal presence of the heavenly Bridegroom. Yea, it will bring to Jesus His Kingdom, Crown and Throne.

CHAPTER SEVEN

THE SECOND COMING OF CHRIST

Charles H. Spurgeon

Four Great Events, and a Fifth—His Promised Return—Necessary—Unquestionably Asserted—What can Hinder it?—When?—Vividly Realized—Seen of All—Denying, Living, Looking—Be Ready—Waiting Patiently—Notion of Delay Harmful

FOUR GREAT EVENTS shine out brightly in our Savior's story. All Christian minds delight to dwell upon His birth, His death, His resurrection, and His ascension. These make four rounds in that ladder of light, the foot of which is upon the earth, but the top whereof reaches to Heaven.

We could not afford to dispense with any one of those four events, nor would it be profitable for us to forget or underestimate the value of any one of them.

> That the Son of God was born of a woman creates in us the intense delight of a brotherhood springing out of a common humanity.
>
> That Jesus once suffered unto the death for our sins, and thereby made a full atonement for us, is the rest and life of our spirit. The manger and the cross together are divine seals of love.
>
> That the Lord Jesus rose again from the dead is the warrant of our justification, and also a transcendently delightful assurance of the resurrection of all His people, and of their eternal life in Him.

Hath He not said, "Because I live, ye shall live also"? The resurrection of Christ is the morning star of our future glory. Equally delightful is the remembrance of His ascension. No song is sweeter than this,—"Thou hast ascended on high; thou hast led captivity captive; thou hast received gifts for men, yea, for the rebellious also, that the Lord God might dwell among them."

Each one of those four events points to another, and they all lead up to it. The fifth link in the golden chain is our Lord's second and most glorious advent. Little is mentioned between His ascent and His descent. True, a rich history comes between; but it lies in a valley between two stupendous mountains: we step from alp to alp as we journey in meditation from the ascension to the second advent.

I say that each of the previous four events points to it. Had He not come a first time in humiliation, born under the law, He could not have come a second time in amazing glory "without a sin offering unto salvation." Because He died once, we rejoice that He dieth no more. Death hath no more dominion over Him, and therefore He cometh to destroy that last enemy whom He hath already conquered.

It is our joy, as we think of our Redeemer as risen, to feel that in consequence of His rising, the trump of the archangel shall assuredly sound for the awaking of all His slumbering people, when the Lord Himself shall descend from Heaven with a shout.

As for His ascension, He could not a second time descend if He had not first ascended; but having perfumed Heaven with His presence, and prepared a place for His people, we may fitly expect that He will come again and receive us unto Himself, that where He is there we may be also.

THE LORD WILL COME AGAIN

He will come again, for *He has promised to return*. We have His own word for it. That is our first reason for expecting Him. Among the last of the words which He spoke to His servant John are these, "Surely I come quickly." You may read it, "*I am coming quickly. I am even now upon the road. I am traveling as fast as wisdom allows. I am always coming, and coming quickly.*"

Some try to explain the Second Coming of Christ as though it meant the believer dying. You may, if you like, consider that Christ comes to His saints in death. In a certain sense He does; but that sense will never bear out the full meaning of the teaching of the Second Advent with which the Scripture is full. No; "the Lord Himself shall descend from heaven with a shout, with the voice of the archangel, and with the trump of God."

Christ will as certainly be here again in glory as He once was here in shame. He often assured His disciples that if He went away from them, He would come again to them; and He left us the Lord's Supper as a parting token to be observed until He comes. As often as we break bread we are reminded of the fact that, though it is a most blessed ordinance, yet it is a temporary one, and will cease to be celebrated when our absent Lord is once again present with us.

He promised to die on the cross, and to rise again the third day: and He kept His word. Let us believe His promise to return again.

Moreover, *the great scheme of redemption requires Christ's return*. It is a part of that scheme that as:

He came once with a sin offering, He should come a second time without a sin offering; that as

He came once to redeem, He should come a second time to claim the inheritance which He has so dearly bought.

He came once that His heel might be bruised; He comes again to bruise the serpent's head, and with a rod of iron to dash His enemies in pieces, as potter's vessels.

He came once to wear the crown of thorns; He must come again to wear the diadem of universal dominion.

He comes to the marriage supper. He comes to gather His saints together.

He comes to glorify them with Himself on this same earth where once He and they were despised and rejected of men.

Make you sure of this, that the whole drama of redemption cannot be perfected without this last act of the coming of their King.

The complete history of Paradise Regained requires that the New Jerusalem should come down from God out of Heaven, prepared as a bride adorned for her husband; and it also requires that the heavenly Bridegroom should come riding forth on His white horse, conquering and to conquer, King of kings and Lord of lords, amid the everlasting hallelujahs of saints and angels. It must be so. The man of Nazareth will come again.

None shall spit in His face then, but every knee shall bow before Him. The Crucified shall come again, and though the nail prints will be visible, no nails shall then fasten His dear hands to the tree; but instead thereof, He shall grasp the scepter of universal sovereignty, and He shall reign forever and ever. Hallelujah!

And next, *it is unquestionably asserted.* "Behold, He cometh." It is not, "Perhaps He will come"; or, "Peradventure He may yet appear." "Behold, He cometh" is dogmatically asserted as an absolute certainty, which was realized by the heart of the man who proclaims it. "Behold, He cometh." All the prophets say that He will come. From Enoch down to the last that spoke by inspiration, they declare, "The Lord cometh with ten thousands of His saints."

You shall not find one who has spoken by the authority of God, who does not, either directly or by implication, assert the coming of the Son of Man, when the multitudes born of woman shall be summoned to His bar, to receive the recompense of their deeds. All the promises are travailing with this prognostication, "Behold, He cometh."

What is there to hinder Christ from coming? When I have studied and thought over this word, "Behold, He cometh," "Yes," I have said to myself, "indeed He does. Who shall hold Him back? His heart is with His church on earth. In the place where He fought the battle He desires to celebrate the victory. His delights are with the sons of men. All His saints are waiting for the day of His appearing, and He is waiting also.

The very earth in her sorrow and her groaning travaileth for His coming, which is to be her redemption. The creation is made subject to vanity for a little while; but when the Lord shall come again, the creation itself also shall be delivered from the bondage of corruption into the glorious liberty of the children of God."

We might question whether He would come a second time if He had not already come the first time; but if He came to Bethlehem, be assured that His feet shall yet stand upon Olivet. If He came to die, doubt not that He will come to reign. If He came to be despised and rejected of men, why should we doubt that He will come to be admired in all them that believe?

WHEN?

When will He come? Ah, that is the question, the question of questions! He will come in His own time. He will come in due time.

A brother minister, calling upon me, said, as we sat together.

"I should like to ask you a lot of questions about the future."

"Oh, well!" I replied, "I cannot answer you, for I daresay I know no more about ii than you do."

"But," said he, "what about the Lord's Second Advent? Will there not be the millennium first?"

I said, "*I cannot tell whether there will be the millennium first; but this I know, the Scripture has left the whole matter, as far as I can see, with an intentional indistinctness, that we may be always expecting Christ to come, and that we may be watching for His coming at any hour and every hour. I think that the millennium will commence after His coming, and not before it. I cannot imagine the kingdom with the King absent. It seems to me to be an essential part of the millennial glory that the King shall then be revealed; at the same time, I am not going to lay down anything definite upon that point. He may not come for a thousand years; He may come tonight. The teaching of Scripture is, first of all, 'in such an hour as ye think not, the Son of Man cometh.' It is clear that, if it were revealed that a thousand years must elapse before He would come, we might very well go to sleep for that time, for we should have no reason to expect that He would come when Scripture told us He would not.*"

"Well," answered my friend, "but when Christ comes, that will be the general judgment, will it not?"

Then I quoted these texts: "The dead in Christ shall rise first"; "But the rest of the dead lived not again until the thousand years were finished. This is the first resurrection."

I said, "There is a resurrection from among the dead to which the Apostle Paul labored to attain.

We shall all rise; but the righteous shall rise a thousand years before the ungodly. There is to be that interval of time between the one and the other; whether that is the millennial glory, or not, this deponent sayeth not, though he thinks it is. But this is the main point, the Lord shall come.

The Second Coming Of Christ

We know not when we are to expect His coming. We are not to lay down as absolutely fixed, any definite prediction or circumstance that would allow us to go to sleep until that prediction was fulfilled, or that circumstance was apparent."

"Will not the Jews be converted to Christ, and restored to their land?" inquired my friend.

I replied, "Yes, I think so. Surely they shall look on Him whom they have pierced, and they shall mourn for Him, as one mourneth for his only son; and God shall give them the kingdom and the glory, for they are His people, whom He has not for ever cast away. The Jews, who are the natural olive branches, shall yet be grafted into their own olive tree again, and then shall be the fullness of the Gentiles."

"Will that be before Christ comes, or after?" asked my friend.

I answered, "I think it will be after He comes; but whether or no, I am not going to commit myself to any definite opinion on the subject."

To you, my friends, I say,—Read for yourselves, and search for yourselves; for still this stands first, and is the only thing that I will insist upon, the Lord will come. He may come now; He may come tomorrow; He may come in the first watch of the night, or the second watch, or He may wait until the morning watch.

But the one word that He gives to us all is, "Watch! Watch! Watch!" that whenever He shall come, we may be ready to open to Him, and to say, in the language of the hymn,

Hallelujah!
Welcome, welcome, Judge divine!

So far I know that we are Scriptural, and therefore perfectly safe in our statements about the Lord's Second Advent.

HIS COMING IS TO BE VIVIDLY REALIZED

I think I see the Apostle John. He is in the spirit; but on a sudden he seems startled into a keener and more solemn attention. His mind is more awake than usual, though he was ever a man of bright eyes that saw afar. We always liken him to the eagle for the height of his flight and the keenness of his vision; yet on a sudden, even he seems startled with a more astounding vision.

He cries out, "Behold! Behold!" He has caught sight of his Lord. He says not, "He will come by-and-by," but, "I can see Him. He is now coming." He has evidently realized the Second Advent.

He has so conceived of the second coming of the Lord that it has become a matter of fact to him; a matter to be spoken of, and even to be written down. "Behold, He cometh!" Have you and I ever realized the coming of Christ so fully as this?

Brothers and sisters, to this realization I invite you. I wish that we could go together in this, until as we went out of the house we said to one another, "Behold, He cometh!" One said to his fellow, after the Lord had risen, "The Lord has risen indeed." I want you now to feel just as certain that the Lord is coming indeed, and I would have you say as much to one another.

SEEN OF ALL

"Behold, He cometh with clouds, and every eye shall see Him, and they also which pierced Him."

I gather from this expression that *it will be a literal appearing and an actual sight.* If the Second Advent was to be a spiritual manifestation, to be perceived by the minds of men, the phraseology would be, "Every mind shall perceive Him." But it is not so: we read, "Every eye shall see Him." Now, the mind can behold the spiritual, but the eye can only see that which is distinctly material and visible.

The Lord Jesus Christ will not come spiritually, for in that sense He is always here; but He will come really and substantially, for every eye shall see Him, even those unspiritual eyes which gazed on Him with hate, and pierced Him. Go not away and dream, and say to yourself, "Oh, there is some spiritual meaning about all this." Do not destroy the teaching of the Holy Ghost by the idea that there will be a spiritual manifestation of the Christ of God, but that a literal appearing is out of the question. That would be altering the record.

The Lord Jesus shall come to earth a second time as literally as He has come a first time. The same Christ who ate a piece of broiled fish and of a honeycomb after He had risen from the dead; the same who said, "Handle me, and see; for a spirit hath not flesh and bones, as ye see me have" — this same Jesus with a material body, is to come in the clouds of Heaven. In the same manner as He went up, He shall come down. He shall be literally seen. The words cannot be honestly read in any other way.

"Every eye shall see Him." Yes, I do literally expect to see my Lord Jesus with these eyes of mine, even as that saint Job expected, who long ago fell asleep, believing that though the worms devour his body, yet in his flesh should he see God, whom his eyes should see for himself, and not another. There will be a real resurrection of the body, though the moderns doubt it; such a resurrection that we shall see Jesus with our own eyes.

We shall not find ourselves in a shadowy, dreamy land of floating fictions, where we may perceive, but cannot see. We shall not be airy nothings, mysterious, vague, impalpable; but we shall literally see our glorious Lord, whose appearing will be no phantom show or shadow dance.

Never day more real than the Day of Judgment; never sight more true than the Son of Man upon the throne of His glory. Will you take this statement home, that you may feel the force of it? We are getting too far away from facts nowadays, and too much into the realm of myths and notions. "Every eye shall see Him"; in this there shall be no delusion.

Note well that *He is to be seen of all kinds of living men*: every eye shall see Him: the king and; the peasant, the most learned and the most ignorant. Those that were blind before shall see when He appears. I remember a man born blind who loved our Lord most intensely, and he was wont to glory in this that his eyes had been reserved for his Lord. He said, "The first whom I shall ever see will be the Lord Jesus Christ. The first sight that greets my newly-opened eyes will be the Son of man in His glory."

Small pleasure is this to eyes that are full of filthiness and pride: they care not for this sight, and yet they must see it whether they please or do not please. They have hitherto shut their eyes to good things but when Jesus comes they must see Him. They will not be able to hide themselves, nor to hide Him from their eyes. They will dread the sight, but it will come upon them, even as the sun shines upon the thief who delights in the darkness. They will be obliged to own in dismay that they behold the Son of Man: they will be so overwhelmed with the sight that there will be no denying it.

He will be seen of those who have been long since dead. What a sight that will be for Judas, and for Pilate, and for Caiaphas, and for Herod! What a sight it will be for those who, in their lifetime, said that there was no Savior, and no need of one; or that Jesus was a mere man, and that His blood was not a propitiation for sin!

Those that scoffed and reviled Him have long since died, but they shall all rise again, and rise to this heritage among the rest that they shall see Him whom they blasphemed sitting in the clouds of Heaven. Prisoners are troubled at the sight of the judge. The trumpet of assize brings no music to the ears of criminals. But thou must hear it, O impenitent sinner!

Even in your grave you must hear the voice of the Son of God, and live, and come forth from the tomb, to receive the things done in thy body, whether they were good or bad. Death cannot hide thee, nor the vault conceal thee, nor rottenness and corruption deliver thee. Thou art bound to see in thy body the Lord who will judge both thee and thy fellows.

DENYING—LIVING—LOOKING

We read in Scripture:

> "The grace of God that bringeth salvation hath appeared to all men; teaching us that, denying ungodliness and worldly lusts, we should live soberly, righteously, and godly in this present world; looking for that blessed hope, and the glorious appearing of the great God and our Savior Jesus Christ; who gave Himself for us, that He might redeem us from all iniquity, and purify unto Himself a peculiar people, zealous of good works."

You see there are three words before you—denying, living, looking.

When the Holy Spirit comes into the heart, He finds that we are conceited, puffed up. We have learned lessons of worldly wisdom and carnal policy, which we need to unlearn and deny.

What have we to deny? First, we have to deny ungodliness. That is a lesson which many of you have great need to learn. Listen to the workingman:

"Oh," they say, "we have to work hard, we cannot think about God or religion."

This is ungodliness! The grace of God teaches us to deny this; we come to loathe such atheism.

Others are prospering in the world, and they cry, "If you had as much business to look after as I have you would have no time to think about your soul or another world. Trying to battle with the competition of the times leaves me no opportunity for prayer or Bible-reading; I have enough to do with my daybook and ledger."

This also is ungodliness! The grace of God leads us to deny this; we abhor such forgetfulness of God. God cannot be forgotten with impunity. If we treat Him as if He were nothing, and leave Him out of our calculations for life, we shall make a fatal mistake.

O my hearer, there is a God, and as surely as you live, you are accountable to Him. When the Spirit of God comes with the grace of the Gospel, He removes our inveterate ungodliness, and causes us to deny it with joyful earnestness.

We next deny "worldly lusts"; that is, the lusts or the present world or age. The lust of the eye, the lust of the flesh, and the pride of life are yet with us. Wherever the grace of God comes effectually,

It makes the loose liver deny the desires of the flesh;
It causes the man who lusted after gold to conquer his greediness;
It brings the proud man away from his ambitions;
It trains the idler to diligence;
It sobers the wanton mind which cared only for the frivolities of life.

The grace of God has made us deny the prevailing philosophies, glories, maxims and fashions of this present world.

But then, brethren, you. cannot be complete with a merely negative religion; you must have something positive; and so the next word is living—that "we should live soberly, righteously, and godly, in this present world."

Observe, brethren, that the Holy Ghost expects us to live in this present world, and therefore we are not to exclude ourselves from it. This age is the battlefield in which the soldier of Christ is to fight. Society is the place in which Christianity is to exhibit the graces of Christ. It is of no use for you to scheme to escape from it. You are bound to breast this torrent, and buffet all its waves. If the grace of God is in you, that grace is meant to be displayed, not in a select and secluded retreat, but in this present world.

This life is described in a threefold way. You are, first, to live "soberly"—that is, for yourself. "Soberly" in all your eating and your drinking, and in the indulgence of all bodily appetites—that goes without saying. You are to live soberly in all your thinking, all your speaking, all your acting. There is to be sobriety in all your worldly pursuits. You are to have yourself well in hand; you are to be self-restrained.

The man who is disciplined by the grace of God becomes thoughtful, considerate, self-contained; and he is no longer tossed about by passion, or swayed by prejudice. As to his fellowman the believer lives "righteously." I cannot understand that Christian who can do a dirty thing in business.

If you mean to go the way of the devil, say so, and take the consequences, but if you profess to be servants of God, deny all partnership with unrighteousness. Dishonesty and falsehood are the opposites of godliness. A Christian man may be poor, but he must live righteously; he may lack sharpness, but he must not lack integrity. A Christian profession without uprightness is a lie. Grace must discipline us to righteous living.

Toward God we are told that we are to be godly. Every man who has the grace of God in him indeed and of a truth, will think much of God, and will seek first the kingdom of God and His righteousness.

God will enter into all his calculations,
God's presence will be his joy,
God's strength will be his confidence,
God's providence will be his inheritance,
God's glory will be the chief end of his being,
God's law the guide of his conversation.

The Second Coming Of Christ

Now, if the grace of God, which has appeared so plainly to all men, has really come with its sacred discipline upon us, it is teaching us to live in this threefold manner.

Once more, there is looking, as well as living. One work of the grace of God is to cause us to be "looking for that blessed hope of the glorious appearing of the great God and our Savior Jesus Christ."

This hope is not of debt, but of grace; though our Lord will give us a reward, it will not be according to the law of works. The Lord cometh, and in the coming of the Lord lies the great hope of the believer, his great stimulus to overcome evil, his main incentive to perfect holiness in the fear of the Lord. Oh, to be found blameless in the day of the manifestation of our Lord! God grant us this!

BE READY

I beg you to get ready to meet our returning Lord. What is the way to be ready to meet Jesus?

- If it is the same Jesus that went away from us who is coming, then let us be doing what He was doing before He went away.
- If it is the same Jesus that is coming, we cannot possibly put ourselves into a posture of which He will better approve than by going about, doing good.
- If you would meet Him with joy, serve Him with earnestness.
- If the Lord Jesus Christ were to come today I should like Him to find me at my studying, praying, or preaching.

Would you not like Him to find you in your Sunday school, in your class, or out there at the corner of the street preaching, or doing whatever you have the privilege of doing in His name? Would you meet your Lord in idleness? Do not think of it.

I called one day on one of my church members, and she was whitening the front steps. She got up all in confusion, and said: "Oh dear, sir, I did not know you were coming today, or I would have been ready."

I replied, "Dear friend, you could not be in better trim than you are; you are doing your duty like a good housewife, and may God bless you."

She had no money to spare for a servant, and she was doing her duty by keeping the home tidy. I thought she looked more beautiful with her pail beside her than if she had been dressed according to the latest fashion. I said to her: "When the Lord Jesus Christ comes suddenly, I hope He will find me doing as you were doing, namely, fulfilling the duty of the hour."

I want you all to get to your pails without being ashamed of them. Serve the Lord in some way or other. Serve Him always. Serve Him intensely. Serve Him more and more.

> Go tomorrow and serve the Lord at the counter, or in the workshop, or in the field.
> Go and serve the Lord by helping the poor and the needy, the widow and the fatherless.
> Go and Serve Him by teaching the children, especially by endeavoring to train your own children.
> Go and show the drunkard that there is hope for him in Christ, or let the fallen woman know that Jesus can restore her.

Do what Jesus has given you the power to do.

THE DELAY

But *the notion of the delay of Christ's coming is always harmful*, however you arrive at it, whether it be by studying prophecy, or in any other way.

> "If that servant say in his heart, My lord delayeth his coming; and shall begin to beat the menservants and maiden, and to eat and drink, and to be drunken; the lord of that servant will come in a day when he looketh not for him, and at an hour when he is not aware, and will cut him in sunder, and will appoint him his portion with the unbelievers."

Do not, therefore, get the idea that the Lord delayeth His coming, and that He will not or cannot come as yet. Far better would it be for you to stand on the tiptoe of expectation, and to be rather disappointed to think that He does not come.

I do not wish you to be shaken in mind so as to act fanatically or foolishly, as certain people did when they went out in the woods with ascension-dresses on, so as to go straight up all of a sudden. Fall into none of those absurd ideas that have led people to leave a chair vacant at the table, and put an empty plate, because the Lord might come and want it; and try to avoid all other superstitious nonsense. To stand stargazing at the prophecies, with your mouth wide open, is just the wrong thing. Far better will it be to go on working for your Lord getting yourself and your service ready for His appearing, and cheering yourself all the while with this thought:

> "While I am at work, my Master may come. Before I get weary, my Master may return. While others are mocking at me, my Master may appear; and whether they mock or applaud, is nothing to me. I live before the great Taskmaster's eye, and do my service knowing that He sees me, and expecting that by-and-by He will reveal Himself to me, and then He will reveal me and my right intention to misrepresenting men."

May the Lord keep you waiting, working, watching, that when He comes, you may have the blessedness of entering upon some larger, higher, nobler service than you could accomplish now, for which you are preparing by the lowlier and more arduous service of this world! God bless you, beloved, and if you do not know my Lord, and therefore do not look for His appearing, remember that He will come whether you look for Him or not; and when He comes you will have to stand at His bar.

One of the events that will follow His coming will be your being summoned before His judgment seat, and how will you answer Him then? How will you answer Him if you refused His love, and turned a deaf ear to the invitations of His mercy? If you have delayed, and delayed, and delayed, and delayed, how will you answer Him? If you stand speechless, your silence will condemn you, and the King will say, "Bind him hand and foot and take him away."

God grant that we may all believe in the Lord Jesus unto life eternal, and then wait for His appearing from Heaven, for His love's sake! Amen.

CHAPTER EIGHT

THE MISSING ONES

J. W.

ONE SUMMER EVENING, for a part of our family worship, I read the fourth chapter of I Thessalonians. Before retiring to rest I seated myself on my easy chair, and mused on the last few verses of the chapter, which were as follows:

> "For if we believe that Jesus died and rose again, even so them also which sleep in Jesus will God bring with Him. For this we say unto you by the word of the Lord, that we which are alive and remain unto the coming of the Lord shall not prevent them which are asleep.
>
> For the Lord Himself shall descend from heaven with a shout, with the voice of the archangel, and with the trump of God; and the dead in Christ shall rise first; then we which are alive and remain shall be caught up together with them in the clouds, to meet the Lord in the air; and so shall we ever be with the Lord."

And as I mused, I fell into a deep sleep, and had a most wonderful dream. My mind seemed to be clear and distinct, and my intellectual faculties stronger and brighter than in my wakeful condition.

I thought I had awakened in the morning, and was somewhat surprised to find that my wife was not beside me as usual. Supposing, however, that her absence was but temporary, I waited, expecting her speedy return; but after the lapse of what I considered a reasonable time, as she did not make her appearance, I arose and dressed.

My wife's apparel was where she had placed it on retiring, and I felt confident she was somewhere about the house. So I went to my daughter Julia's room, thinking she might know the whereabouts of her mother; but after knocking several times without response, I entered, and found that she was also missing.

"Strange, passing strange," said I to myself; "where can they both be?"

Then I went to the room of our son Frank, and found him up and already dressed, which was something quite unusual for him at an hour so early. He said he had passed a very restless night, and thought he might better get up.

I told him of the absence of his mother and sister from their rooms, and requested him to look around and see if he could find them. In the meantime I hurriedly finished dressing, and soon Frank returned and said the missing ones were nowhere to be found, and that every door leading outward was securely locked, as on the preceding evening. We were at our wit's end, and what to make of this strange occurrence we did not know.

On again visiting Julia's room we found on a stand her well-marked open Bible. One prominent verse attracted my attention, it read:

"Be ye also ready, for *in such an hour as ye think not the Son of Man cometh*."

This passage, my wife had always declared, referred to the coming of Christ for His saints, the redeemed Church, while I insisted that it meant only the preparation for death. But I am digressing. Frank and I concluded that, without waiting for breakfast, we should each take a different route, and visit some of our most intimate friends in quest of our dear ones.

I first called on my wife's sister, Mrs. E., who, with her husband, were good, respectable people, members of a Christian Church, though rather world-minded. After I had rung the bell several times, and waited somewhat impatiently, she appeared, and apologized for her tardiness by saying that she was in a "peck of trouble," and had to prepare breakfast herself, for her servant girl, whom she had always considered to be a real good Christian, had played her a mean trick.

"She has gone off somewhere, without even putting the kettle on the range, or saying a word to any of us. But what puzzles us to know is how she got out of the house, for the doors are all locked and the keys inside, just as we left them last evening on our return from Mrs. B.'s progressive euchre party."

"Indeed," said I, "it is exceeding strange," and then I explained to her the object of my morning visit.

When she heard of the mysterious absence of my wife and Julia she became so very nervous that I was glad to change the subject by saying that, as I had not breakfasted, I would join them in their morning repast. When her husband heard my story he treated it with a good deal of levity, and declared that my wife was only playing me a practical joke, to induce me to rise earlier in the morning. He was sure the missing ones had secreted themselves somewhere about the house, and when I returned home I would find them all right.

As we seated ourselves at the table, Mrs. E. said we would have to take coffee without milk, as her milkman, who had heretofore been very reliable, had failed to make his appearance.

Presently the doorbell rang, and Frank entered in a state of great nervous excitement, saying he had been all over inquiring for his mother, and that in almost every house he found trouble similar to our own. Almost everyone was anxiously searching for missing ones. He also stated that the streets were thronged with excited people, hurrying to and fro, many of them weeping bitterly.

Breakfast was scarcely over before inquiries were made at the door as to missing neighbors, and among those who called was Mr. H., who greatly astonished us by stating that his two youngest children, ten and twelve years of age, had gone off with their grandmother, who had been bedridden for over six years. At this announcement Mr. E. showed evident signs of alarm, and related a conversation he had held yesterday with a friend, whose religious ideas he had looked upon as quite heretical.

His friend insisted that a vast majority of church members in these days were but nominal Christians, "lovers of pleasure more than lovers of God," and that the love of the masses for religious things had reached a very low ebb.

"My friend also assured me," said Mr. E., "that the Scriptures clearly taught that when the elect number of Christ's Church would be complete, Christ would come as unexpectedly as a thief in the night, and call His saints, both dead and alive, to meet Him in the air. The transformation would be effected in the twinkling of an eye; and although the call would be made with a shout and the sound of a trumpet, yet none would hear it but those for whom it was intended. Then would be realized the import of Christ's words: 'In that night there shall be two in one bed; the one shall be taken and the other left, Two shall be grinding at the mill; the one shall be taken and the other left.' I fear that time has now come, and sad to say, we are among the left ones!"

Now as the morning was far advanced it was suggested that we go down to our business places. Frank had already gone to his office, and I, with a heavy heart, wended my way along the avenue among an unusual throng of men and women, whose faces betokened intense sorrow.

In the business parts of the city I observed that many stores were closed, and that those that were open did not appear to be doing any business. Every tavern that I passed was open, as usual, with groups of men outside, apparently engaged in serious discussion. As I passed by the City Hall, there was no perceptible diminution of the usual crowd of political "hangers-on" around the building.

When I reached my own store, I found that my bookkeeper, and the faithful old porter who had served me so many years, had not yet put in an appearance. My two other clerks were on hand, doing nothing; nor did I feel like asking them to do anything. I then went to the Chamber of Commerce, and found the largest gathering of merchants that I had seen there in many months.

Instead of the lively, noisy bustle of buying and selling, and clerks and messenger boys running to and fro, there was a solemn gloom pervading the whole assembly. By unanimous consent, and in consequence of the great calamity that had overtaken the community, it was voted that "three days" grace be allowed on all contracts falling due this day."

I will not attempt to set forth any of the reasons and speculations that were advanced as to the cause of our present troubles, but all agreed that the visitation was a supernatural one, and that in some way we who were left on the earth were blamable for it.

In the afternoon, by common consent, business of all kinds was suspended, except in the vicinity of the taverns, where a great deal of disorder prevailed. Here and there were groups of people in earnest conversation. At one of them was a man who seemed to be well-versed in Scripture, and as I approached he was saying:

"This is the day spoken of by Christ, but none of us believed it, and now we are beginning to realize how foolish we were."

In the evening nearly every church in the city was open, with overflowing congregations. Everybody was anxious to know the cause and meaning of the "great visitation," and to learn how lost hopes might be regained. Many of the pastors had gone with the missing ones, but some were present in their churches. All order of service was dispensed with, and noisy confusion prevailed.

Crimination and recrimination were bandied to and fro between the pastors and the people, the latter asserting that if the pastors had done their duty, and taught their flocks the plain truths of the Bible, instead of lulling them to sleep with philosophical and moral essays, they would not now be in their present sad condition. In my own church the pastor was present, with scores of persons whom I had but rarely seen at meetings.

Most of the active workers and constant worshipers were absent. Audible groans and deep drawn sighs were occasionally heard from various parts of the room. Some were bemoaning the loss of children, others of husbands, of wives, of fathers and mothers.

The pastor was speaking when I entered the room, and was entreating the audience to endeavor to allay their feelings. He said:

"None of you realize the keen disappointment I experience at this result of my labors. I am accused of having preached too much about the affairs of this life, and too little about the heavenly state, and the things to come; and of having kept you in ignorance of the imminency of the awful visitation which has manifested itself among us this day. In reply to these accusations I can only say that I have taught you the same theology that was taught to me in college, namely to treat the Bible as a book largely of spiritual symbols and allegories.

"But I now confess that I was sadly mistaken, for, after what has occurred, I cannot help believing that *God's Word means just what it says.* I am glad, however, now to be able to say for your comfort that, since this morning, I have made a prayerful examination of the Scriptures as to our present condition, and find that we are yet in the place of hope."

Here a chorus of voices ejaculated, "Thank God for that!"

The pastor proceeded: "Although we had lost the glorious privilege of the raptured saints, salvation is yet ours, if we humbly and truly accept it. We may have to pass through greater trials and tribulations than the world has ever experienced ere we reach the Kingdom, but he that endureth to the end shall be saved."

Here the electric light suddenly went out, and there arose such fearful screams that *I sprang to my feet in terror—and—awoke*!

My wife, who was in an adjoining room, hearing my sudden uprising, hastened in to see what was the matter. Oh, how glad I was to see her, and to realize that my terrible experience in my easy chair was only a dream! But the more I thought of it afterward, the more solemn seemed the Scripture truths which it contained, and the more was I impressed with the importance of having our lamps trimmed and burning, ready to go out and meet the Bridegroom.

Plan of the Ages

WITH CHART

BY

George C. Needham

EXPLANATORY

HIS presentation of the Ages is a Study. It was therefore not necessary to enlarge upon details. The Bible student is requested to place the Chart before him and carefully compare it with this Exposition; also to give exact examination to every scripture passage.

The practical value of prophetic study should be apparent to all. Christian believers ought to have a right "understanding of the times." Become familiar with the great historical and prophetical landmarks outlined in Chart and Key in order that you may be qualified for further study of the prophetic scriptures.

Plan of The Ages

THE accompanying Chart has been prepared with the view of helping those who desire to study the Prophetic Ages of Scripture. The eye quickly conveys to the mind the Plan of The Ages, according to chart, by successive circles which represent them.

[First the chart images, then the accompanying text will follow:]

Plan of The Ages: With Chart

Single page view:

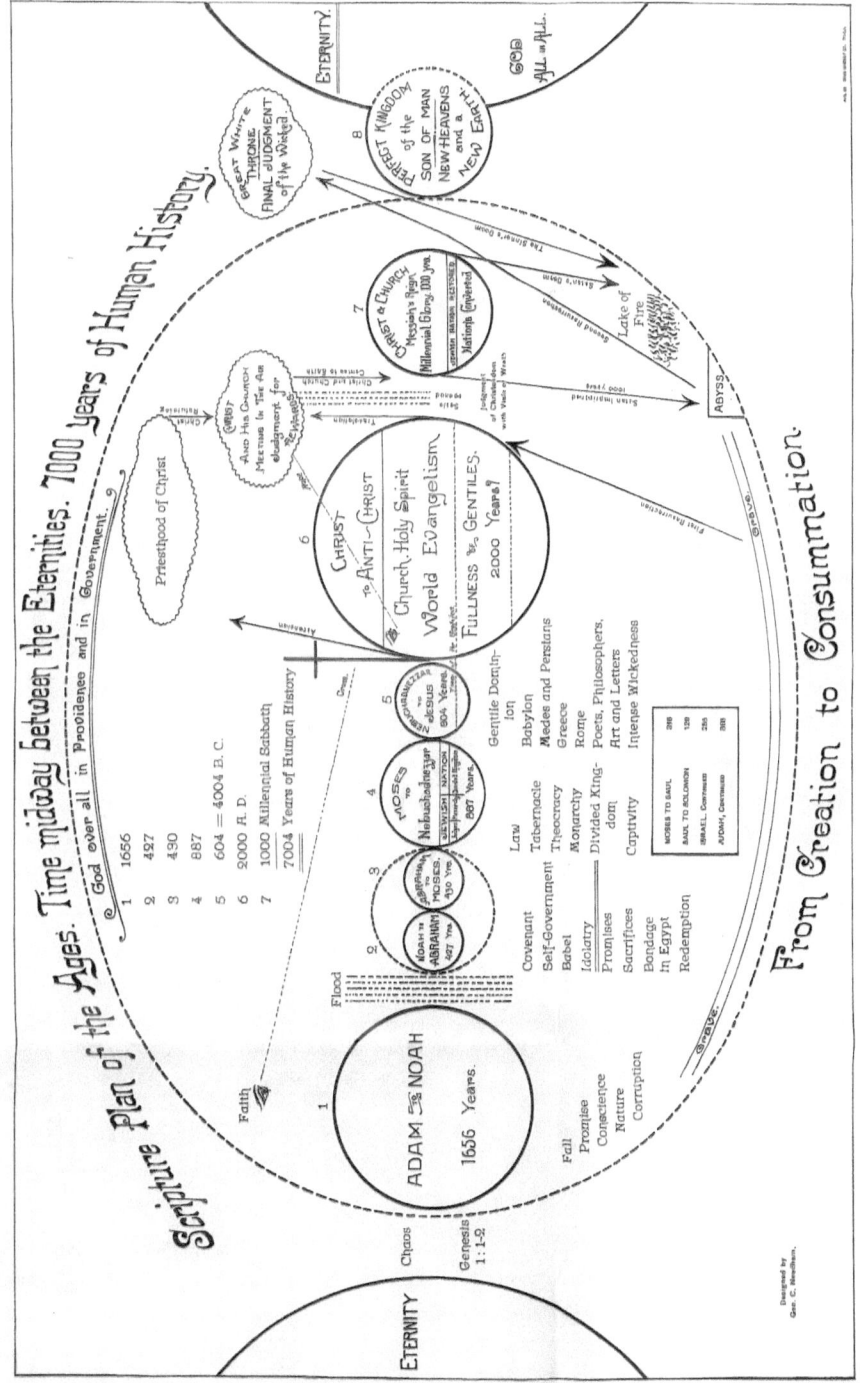

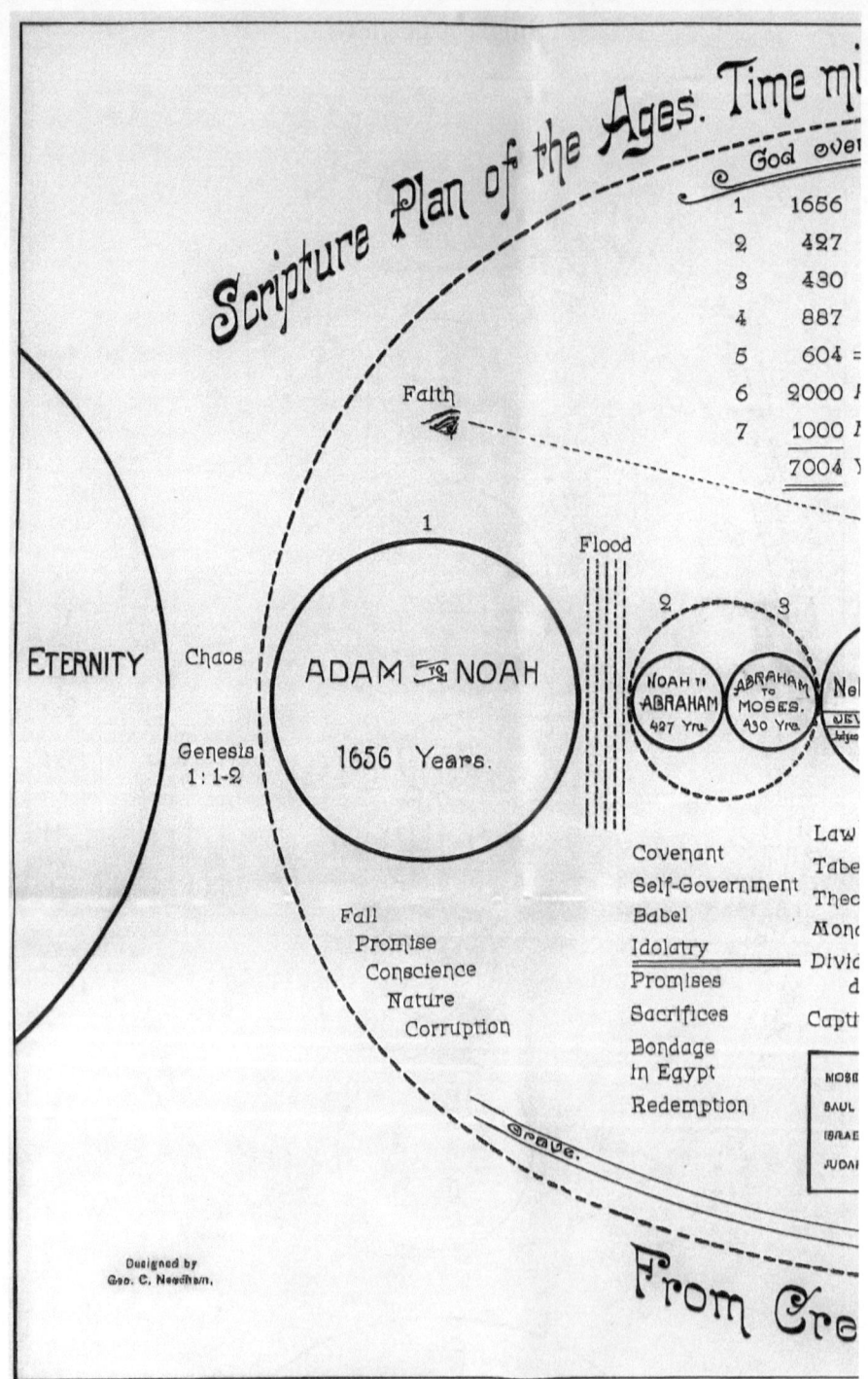

Plan of The Ages: With Chart

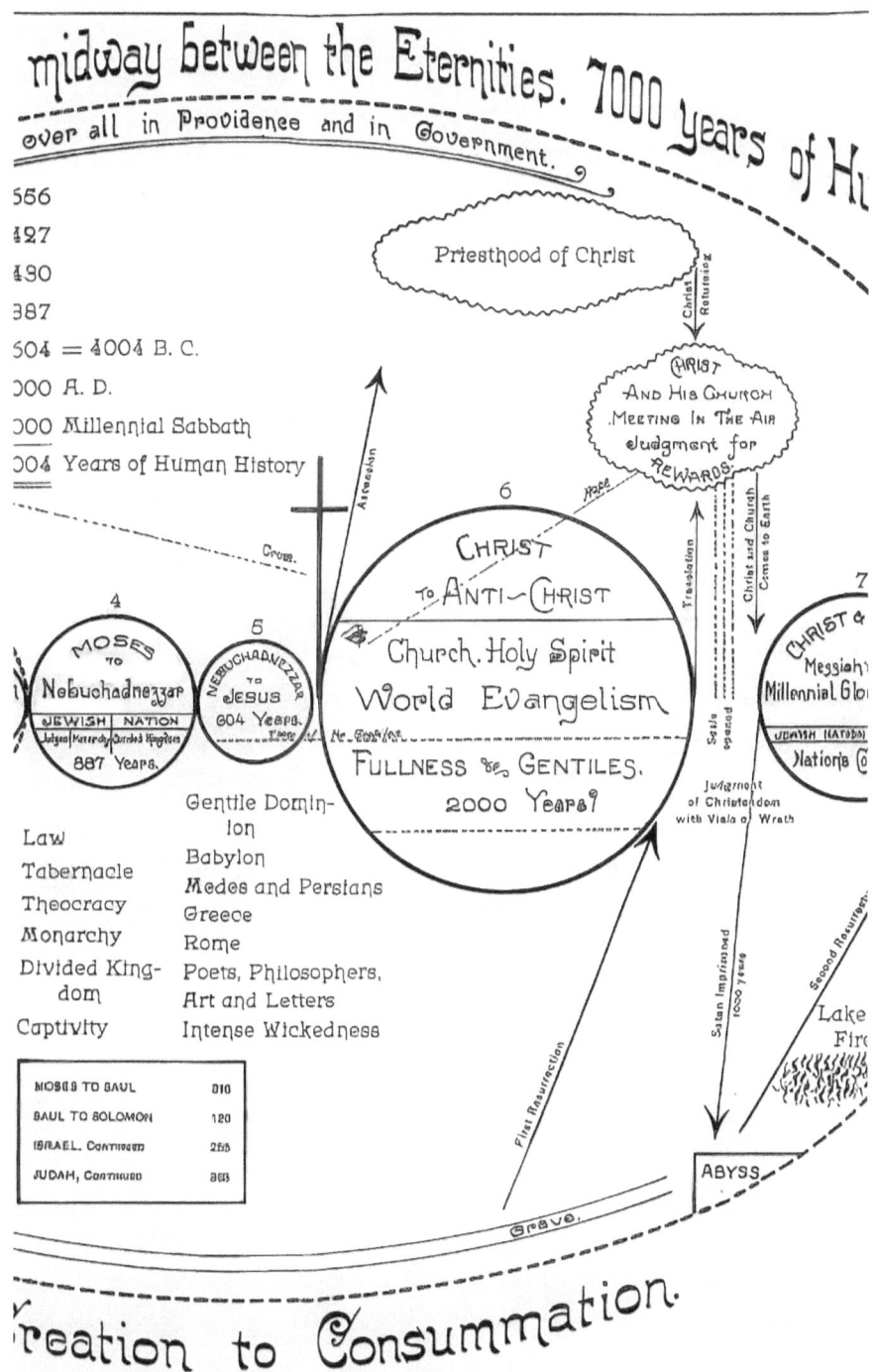

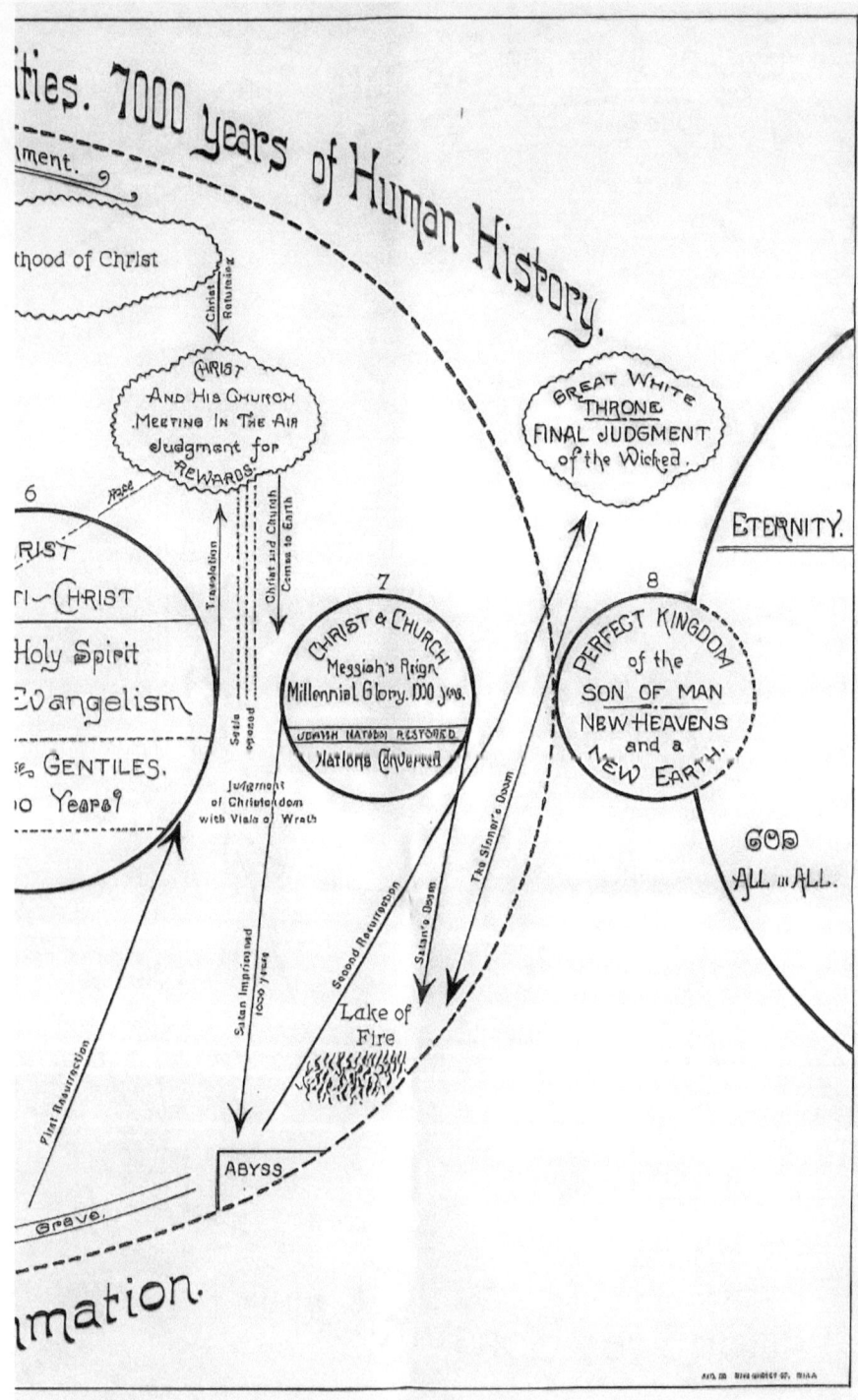

A correct knowledge of Biblical divisions of Time will harmonize prophets and apostles. Prophecy and history are a unit. The Divine Word is always in accord with itself, although its harmonies may not at first be readily perceived. Much mischief has been wrought by confounding distinct Periods of Time, which have their own peculiar characteristics. These are not identical, but successional. Great perplexity has also arisen from not discriminating between "the end of the World," and "the end of, the Age." In fact, the substitution of "World" for "Age" has led to a system of false interpretation, and the texts which have been mis-translated have obscured their real meaning.

The proper translation of the word *AION* is "Age," not "World." For example, in Eph. 2: 7, we read, "in the AGES to come," and in Col. 1:26, "the mystery which had been hid from the AGES," the word is correctly translated.

But in the following instances, as well in other texts, the word "World" is misleading:

Matt. 13: 39, "The harvest is the end of the World (Age)," see also verses 40-49.

Matt. 24:3, "What shall be the sign of thy coming, and of the end of the World (Age)?"

Luke 1:70, "His holy prophets, which have been since the World (Age) began."

1 Cor. 10:11, "They are written for our admonition upon whom the ends of the World (Ages) are come."

Paul stood at the junction of two Ages, the Jewish and the Christian. Heb. 1:2, "by whom also He made the Worlds," should read " constituted the Ages," indicating a plan.

Heb. 9:26, "Now, once in the end of the World (Age) hath He appeared." In the former part of the verse "World" is correct. "For then must He often have suffered since the foundation of the World (kosmos)."

Rom. 16: 25, "Kept secret since the World (Ages) began."

From the above verses, selected out of a great number, it is evident that there has been a succession of Ages from the beginning, and there are Ages yet to come.

Are these Ages in their character, duration, and mission dependent on chance, evolution, or human arrangement? Or are they the result of arbitrary fate? Verily, no! God has had a Plan which He is working out after the counsel of His own will from Creation to Consummation.

From beginning to end the Divine Mind sketched a program of dispensations, which will be executed notwithstanding Satan's effort to thwart, and man's perverse will to oppose.

The Ages are not necessarily of uniform duration, but each one by itself reveals God's goodness and man's wickedness. In every Age the Creator gave ample opportunity with every facility for the race to govern itself, and come back again to Him, but in every instance man proved to be incapable. Deceived by the devil, he plunges onward in a mad course of enmity against God. And had not God interposed in every Age, in the exercise of mercy towards the race, no flesh could be saved. History has forever settled the question that civilization, culture, liberty, or wealth has never elevated the race morally, or brought the human will into harmony with the divine.

"That which is born of the flesh is flesh."

"They that are in the flesh cannot please God."

"Except a man be born from above he cannot see the Kingdom of God."

Let us now examine the Chart. The oval dotted line sweeping around the circles represents time, midway between the ETERNITIES. The arc of a circle to the extreme left indicates the past eternity.

Of this unlimited duration little can be said.

There was God and space, Ps. 90:2. The Trinity was there in solitary grandeur and in eternal councils, Prov. 8:22-32. In Time there was beginning, when the Godhead put forth the almighty fiat, and at His bidding creation appeared. The space between the arc and first circle is chaos. This period of disorder is embraced in Gen. 1:1, 2. If the scientist demands hundreds, thousands, or millions of years for the development of formations, they may be extended during that unknown and unknowable period. In this pamphlet we pay no atten-

Plan of The Ages: With Chart

tion to the conceits of men who disregard God's Word, but who love to juggle with their theoretical problems of Carboniferous, Permian, Paleozoic, Jurassic, Mesozoic, Cenozoic, and Glacial Periods, and who are insanely determined to prove the Bible unscientific, unreliable, and fabulous. We set over against their learned guesses, the simple and sublime words, "The earth was without form and void, and darkness was upon the face of the deep."

After the arrangement of the planet with its elements of land, water, and firmament, and its divisions of kingdoms, with their respective classifications of vegetable and animal life, consummated by the creation of man, the years which embrace the successive Ages are assumed to be limited to seven thousand.

The circles in the Chart show the order of the Ages and their duration. They are numbered 1 to 7 within the oval of Time. No. 8 is conjoined with the Eternal State.

AGE FROM ADAM TO NOAH

IT IS easy to determine the boundaries of this Age of human history. Man appears on the scene fresh from the hand of his Creator. He was made innocent of evil, Godlike in character. Yet was he a free moral agent. The devil appeared against him and by stratagem overcame him. Man sinned; penalties and consequences followed. Children were born to our first parents in the nature of their sinful flesh. As the people multiplied, the race deteriorated. Wickedness prevailed and judgment by a universal flood ended that Age.

During this first sixteen hundred years of human probation man had conscience and nature to guide him, but his depraved will and corrupt heart preferred darkness to light. Therefore, man was without excuse.

Some individuals, such as Abel, Enoch, and Noah, were saved by faith in the Promise. They believed in God.

Their altars and characters proved them to be men above their fellows. In every Age the Just "live by faith."

During this Age many important institutions were established, and great historical events transpired. Yet man degenerated until his iniquities arose to heaven. Then did God rain down judgment upon this filthy race.

Summary:

Man created, Gen. 1:26, 27; 2:7.
Man sinned, Gen. 3:6.
Penalties and consequences, Gen. 3:14-19.
Promise of redemption, Gen. 3:15.
Corruption of the race, Gen. 6:5, 11, 12.
Judgment ends the Age, Gen. 7:17-24.

AGE FROM NOAH TO ABRAHAM

HIS Age has its own marked peculiarities.

The flood which destroyed the race deluged the earth for a year thereafter.

Then did Noah stand at the head of a new people. But sinful, fallen human nature was the same, and the Age of self-government under a covenant, in addition to nature and conscience, produced an unbelieving race, who sought to defy God by building a tower whose top would reach to heaven.

During this period of about four hundred years man again deteriorated morally. Universal idolatry prevailed. The Age of self-government ended, as that principle must ever end, in the deification of man and the rejection of God.

Summary:

Dominion given to Noah, Gen. 9:1, 2.
Principle of self-government, Gen. 9:6.
God's Covenant with Noah, Gen. 13:16.
Man's proposal to build a tower, Gen. 11:4.
Judgment on the unbelievers, Gen. 11:6.

AGE FROM ABRAHAM TO MOSES

THIS Age we find Headship bestowed on Abram. Witnesses for God were few.

The race had become idolatrous. Both Adam and Noah had begun well, but their posterity lapsed into corrupt practices which ended in judgment. Abram was next chosen, called out from an idolatrous family to witness for God by a life of faith. The reality of faith was successfully proven in his career, yet was he not perfect. Perfection is not found in human nature. Nevertheless, the "God of glory" who appeared to Abram was also to him and his posterity the "God of grace." By Covenant and Promise, He sought to bind a people to Himself. Abraham proved loyal. Isaac possessed faith in God, and lived righteously, yet was he inferior to his father in consecration. Jacob was less godly, while his sons in early life betrayed fleshly envy and unnatural cruelty.

Joseph became the savior of his household, but another Pharaoh had arisen through whose agency judgment visited the children of Abraham. Alas, they had departed from the living God, proving again as before that man gravitates sin-ward. Holiness is not the fruit of the natural man. History proves the race under every condition and advantage an entire moral failure. Genesis closes with the suggestive words, "a coffin in Egypt," a type of man's condition morally, not withstanding his seeming greatness; an illustration also of the condition of the Hebrews, from Joseph to Moses.

Summary:

Abram called out, Gen. 12:1, 2; Josh 24: 2.
Promise, Gen. 15:5.
Covenant, Gen. 15 19-18.
Deterioration in patriarchal families, Gen. 12:11-13; 36:7; 25:33; 27-41; 27:20.
Judgment, Exodus 1:13, 14.

The dotted circle embracing Nos. 2 and 3 shows the close relation of these Ages in their Patriarchal character.

AGE FROM MOSES TO NEBUCHADNEZZAR

DOMINION, vested in Adam, in Noah, and in Abraham, now passes into the hands of Moses. He is a deliverer and a reformer. In the first capacity he succeeded; in the second he failed. Not that Moses was inefficient, but the people were per verse. They were weak through the flesh. For nearly 900 years Israel had a national existence. The years of their loyalty to God, and of their sorrow for sin were brief; the years of their wickedness and waywardness were many.

God was patient with them marvelously. The nation was first organized at the base of Mount Sinai. A people formerly homogeneous now became unified. The infant nation must have a government. What shall its form be? If a kingdom, who shall be their king? Who else but Jehovah? Their first form of government was therefore theocratic. Judges under God were their counselors, leaders, and deliverers. For the space of about four hundred years Jehovah was absolute King.

Great was His grace, marvelous His forbearance, amazing His love for a whimsical, erratic, and irritable people. Finally, in their mad caprice, they demanded a man-king. Jehovah allowed it so. Monarchy then began its period of probation. Saul was selected as the best specimen of humanity. In him human nature had its fullest development. Was it God-ward? Alas, no, Saul's insane jealousies; his imperious despotism; his senseless superstitions, and his low, mean trickery proved again the moral depravity of human nature even in its best estate.

David succeeded Saul. He was a man after God's own heart in his official character, and morally was a contrast to Saul, for he sought after the Ford. Grace elevated and purified David.

Solomon came after David. His beginning was wise, his end was folly. Under these three kings the Monarchy of Israel lasted one hundred and twenty years.

Thereafter existed a nation divided against itself. How then should its kingdom stand? Israel, embracing ten tribes, continued two hundred and fifty-five years, when the Assyrians led her into captivity. Judah, comprising two tribes, continued her separate existence for three hundred and eighty-eight years when she was taken captive to Babylon.

Under Ezra and Nehemiah Jerusalem was colonized by remnants of these captives, and during the Maccabean wars those in the land of their fathers made heroic struggle to regain their lost supremacy. But the nation had doomed itself by its iniquities. And when the Messiah came out of Judah, His own people received him not. Then was wrath filled to the uttermost and the nation ceased to be.

Jewish nationality ended in defeat and in judgment. The Jews are now a scattered people, with out a King, without a Throne, without a Temple, without a Priest.

Judgment upon the nation for the present ended their national career. The parallel lines through the circle representing this Age indicate the existence of the nation. The same lines are seen in circle number 7 to show when Israel nationally will be again revived and established.

Summary:

Redemption from Egypt, Ex. Chapters 12 to 15.
National unification, Ex. 12:2.
Announcement of Raw, Ex. 20.
Preparation for sacrifices, Ex. 25.
Theocracy, Ex. 13:17, 18. " God led," Ex. 15:3, 18.
Monarchy, 1 Sam. 8:4-7; 1 Sam. 10:24.
Divided Kingdom, 1 Kings 11:29-43; 12:1-19.
Israel's Captivity, 2 Kings 17:9-12.
Judah's Captivity, 2 Kings 25:1-11.

NEBUCHADNEZZAR TO JESUS

WITH the Babylonian King commenced the "Times of the Gentiles," which continue their course to this day. These "Times" include the governments represented in the Colossus of Nebuchadnezzar's dream (Dan 2). The Babylonian empire was the first universal monarchy under Gentile head ship. The Medo-Persian, Grecian and

Roman followed. The evolution was downward, not upward. From gold to clay marked the de cadence of earthly governments, and the deterioration of human power. The image weakens from one united head of gold to ten toes of clay.

Daniel's vision of Gentile governments (Chap, 7) was that of four beasts, from the noble lion to the mongrel nameless animal, again showing the loss of splendor and of unity. It is significant that Nebuchadnezzar, a wordly [sic] idolater, saw human governments under the figure of a man, while Daniel, a servant of Jehovah, divinely educated, saw them under the figure of beasts. As it was then, so now. The glamour of politics hides the actual, and not until the closing catastrophes of this Age will the majority be compelled to see that the deification of man foreruns his doom. Man in government becomes a ravening beast.

From Nebuchadnezzar to Jesus embraces a period of about six hundred years. Babylonian supremacy, Medo-Persian power and Grecian ascendancy, were developed and destroyed within five hundred and fifty years. During that time the head, breasts and body of the image were formed. About fifty years before Jesus was born the Caesars arose, and but a little while previous to His incarnation was Roman supremacy established. The legs of the Image were not therefore formed, and the smiting of the Colossus by the mystic stone could not have taken place at the time of our Ford's first advent. The legs have since that time extended themselves.

Once united, Rome became divided into Eastern and Western Rome. When every form of government symbolized in the Colossus shall have been tested and proved unstable, then Christ descends with power and great glory to uproot the kingdoms of men and to overthrow the governments of earth. The mystic stone shall fill the whole earth by itself, for the kingdoms of the world shall have become the kingdoms of our Ford and of His Christ.

The dotted lines running through the circles 5 and 6 show the continuance of the "Times of the Gentiles" until the end of this present Age.

Note these facts:

1. The Stone has not yet fallen.
2. The Stone falls in judgment for destruction, not in grace for conversion.
3. The Stone does not absorb the Image into itself, but drives it away.
4. The kingdoms of men, and the Kingdom of God in its complete form, cannot co-exist.
5. The Stone may even now be ready for its crushing descent upon governments autocratic, despotic, monarchic, democratic and Satanic.

I need but refer to the fact that the World morally during that Age had been sinking into a pit of iniquity. Neither the glory of Babylon, the culture of Greece, nor the power of Rome, brought the race back to God. On the contrary, their very poets, philosophers, reformers, scholars and thinkers lapsed into vices indescribable. After four thousand years of human history man, with all that God had done for him was in his latter state worse than his first. "Cease ye from man whose breath is in his nostrils: for wherein is he to be accounted of?"

Summary:

Gentile supremacy, Dan. 2:21, 31-45.
Times of the Gentiles, Duke 21:24.
Gentile human nature depicted, Rom 1:11-32.

AGE FROM CHRIST TO ANTICHRIST

THIS is our own Age; that which affects us chiefly. The Age of the Spirit who abideth with and in the Church; the Age of world-wide evangelism, an Age which should recognize the mission of Jesus, "I am come that they might have life." Four thousand years of experiments and experience have proved man incapable of rising into the higher and spiritual nature. This, work — regeneration and resurrection — Christ came to do. By regeneration man is raised from the death of sin to a life of righteousness, by resurrection shall he be raised to occupy the kingdom which is yet to come.

Earth's sovereignty has been promised to the Church, but her acquisition of it cannot be until the King Himself appears, and she shall be glorified together with Him. But the professing church, composed of a mixed multitude, impatient for do minion, allies herself to the kings of the earth, and becomes intoxicated with her apparent successes. She loves the display of conquest and wickedly glories in her shame. Still within her borders are those who are called and chosen and faithful; believing ones who read rightly the program of the Ages, and are therefore not ignorant of Satan's devices.

The present Age commenced with the rejection of Christ; it will end with the reception of Antichrist. It began when Christ ascended; it will close when He descends again to earth. It was inaugurated by the coming of the Holy Spirit and the formation of the Church, that Body of Christ which only includes the truly saved; it will have run its course when the Church is completed and caught away to meet her returning Lord. It began by displays of Almighty grace to sinners, with announcements of the Gospel of Jesus Christ; it will close with the outpourings of judgments on them that know not God, who refused to obey that Gospel, and who received not the love of the truth that they might be saved.

The peculiarity of the Age is its mixed character. Wheat and tares growing side by side; good fish and bad in the same drag-net; sheep and goats browsing together; wise and foolish virgins slumbering and sleeping-present and prominent features of our times ? Ignorance of God and indifference to spiritual things; lawlessness and insubordination; apostasy, sneering, and scoffing; false philosophies supplanting faith, and speculating sciences antagonizing revelation. Dust of the flesh and laxity of morals, the desecration of everything sacred, including the sabbath, marriage, the home, and public worship. Mountebanks for ministers, and parasites for preachers. Piety has been swept aside while Pride occupies her place. Dove to Christ has waned, while pursuit after a false liberal ism has waxed hotly. Soundness in faith and contention for sound doctrine have been undermined by fashionable skepticism and weakened by the dry-rot of "higher criticism." As our Lord looked down the centuries and saw with prophetic eye the abounding iniquity which would mark the closing days of this Age, sadly, we should imagine, He asked, "When the Son of Man cometh shall He find faith in the earth?" Nevertheless His commission has never been revoked, "Preach the Gospel to every creature," and the light of the Gospel will continue to shine brighter and brighter in every dark land where it finds entrance.

Summary:

This is the Age of the Spirit, John 14:16.
It is not His purpose to convert the World, John 16:8-11.
It is the Day of Salvation, 2 Cor. 6:2.
It is the Day of Grace, John 3:16-19.
It is the Age of Evangelism, Matt. 28:19,20.
It is a mixed Age, Matt. 13.

It will end as the others, in the decadence of an ungodly race, while the real Christian shall he taken away from the evil to come, Matt. 24:36-44.
It will end in Judgment, Luke 21:25-36.

AGE OF CHRIST'S MILLENNIAL KINGDOM

OUR Age will not close the solemn drama enacted upon this planet. For six thousand years Satan has seemed to hold the seat of power. Certainly his hellish work has been universal and unbroken. But the hour will arrive when he shall be defeated.

There will be a space of years between the departure of the Church to meet Christ in the air, and the advent of both to take possession of the earth. During that time Satan will energize the Antichrist with his own awful power, will summon to his aid all the principalities and spirits of darkness, will make another desperate effort to hold possession of the earthly kingdom, and keep the true Heir out of His own inheritance. But in this he shall signally fail. The Son of God will confront him, bind him, and banish him to the abyss, where he will remain imprisoned for one thousand years.

The reader will observe a succession of events crowding together between the closing of our own Age (No. 6) and the beginning of the next (No. 7). Chiefly these:

1. The resurrection of the righteous dead, 1 Thess. 4: 14.
2. The translation of the living saints, 1 Thess. 4:1 7.
3. Reunion of the sleepers and watchers caught up together, 1 Thess. 4. 17.
4. The Meeting in the air between Christ and His glorified Church, 1 Thess. 4:17.
5. Examination of believers for rewards, or the Judgment-seat of Christ, 2 Cor. 5:10; 1 Cor. 3:11-15.
6. Judgments with vials of wrath poured out on the earth, affecting:-

    (1) The Unregenerate who refused the Gospel of Christ, 2 Thess. 1: 7-10; 2: 9-12.
    (2) Jews and others who give their allegiance to Antichrist, Dan. 8:25; Rev. 14:9-1.

7. The Advent of Christ and His Church from the aerial heavens to the earth, Zech. 14:4, 5. Then will take place:

    (1) Destruction of Antichrist and his allies, 2 Thess. 2:8.
    (2) Binding and imprisonment of Satan, Rev. 20:1-3.
    (3) Judgment of nations in governmental character, Matt. 25:31-46.
    (4) Re-establishment of David's Throne with David's royal Son as King in Zion, Duke 1: 32, 33.

The Seventh Age, inaugurated by the personal presence of Christ on earth, will continue 1000 years. It will outshine all other Ages preceding it in universal righteousness. The Glory of God will overshadow it. Converted Israel in her restored national character shall have the supreme place among the nations of the earth. Heathen nations, long enshrouded in pagan darkness, shall hail the King and willingly accept His sovereignty. Yet this blessed Sabbatical era will not be perfect.

Human nature will once more betray its perversity. Satan will have a respite given him. Will he submit to Christ and cease his rebellion? Will he pay homage to the King of kings? Nay, rather shall his hate intensify. He will make a final struggle to regain possession of the planet. He will rally around his black flag every demon, every fallen spirit, every wretched apostate, every subject traitorous to Immanuel, and dash in maddened rage against the holy city. It will be the final conflict between good and evil, righteousness and unrighteousness, heaven and hell, Christ and Satan. But Right will prevail. Jesus will conquer. The devil will be cast into the lake of fire, and all enemies of God shall be destroyed.' The wicked dead shall then be raised for final judgment, the Great White Throne will be set, the books opened, sentence pronounced, its execution speedily administered, and those who offended will be banished forever from the planet into that awful hell prepared for the devil and his angels.

Summary:

There will be a millennium on earth, Rev. 20:4-6.

It will not be the perfect Kingdom, Rev. 20:7-9.

The Glory of God will be here, Isa. 4:5.

The Millennial Kingdom begins when Jesus comes again to earth, Zech. 14: 4.

Our present attitude, Titus 2: 11-13.

AGE OF THE PERFECT KINGDOM OF THE SON OF MAN

WE CANNOT but believe that the prophecies which speak of an Age when Christ shall reign over a renewed earth, and a holy, sinless race, will follow these final judgments. Purgatorial fires will have purified air and earth. Every material element of evil, every spiritual impurity will have forever passed away. No more defilement shall be found within the planet. There shall be "new heavens and a new earth wherein dwelleth righteousness." How long this glorious Bra shall continue we do not know. It is outside the circle of Time, and will merge into the Eternal State, when the Son shall give up a perfected Kingdom to the Father, and God shall be All in All.

Eden re-planted on a universal scale; Paradise restored and extended; Satan conquered, banished, eternally suffering in the quenchless fire; Jesus, Redeemer, King, forever vindicated, glorified, exalted. As glimpses of the eternal future were given to the seer of Patmos he depicted these glories in the glowing chapters which end the book of Revelation. As we stand near the approaching end of our Age and look back beyond the creation of man and of the planet, we confidently believe, "In the beginning, God." As we glance onward to the predicted glories of the future, we reverently exclaim," God All and in All, our God forever and ever, Father, Son, and Spirit, to whom be glory throughout the Ages of the Ages. Amen."

Summary:

1. The Millennial Age will not be the perfected Kingdom of Christ, Zech. 14:16-19; Rev. 20:7-9: Ezekiel 38 chp. and 39 chp.

2. A Kingdom is predicted which shall be absolutely holy, 2 Peter 3:13; Isa. 11:6-9; Hab. 2: 14.

3. It will be a sinless Kingdom without rebels or apostates which Christ will deliver to the Father. Zech. 14:20, 21; Dan. 7:13, 14, 27; 1 Cor. 15:24-28.

(I know that few of my fellow-students advocate an Age between the Millennial Period and the Eternal State, but I request them to carefully re-examine the subject. The above is but a hint.)

www.ingramcontent.com/pod-product-compliance
Lightning Source LLC
Chambersburg PA
CBHW020428010526
44118CB00010B/479